MOYERS ON AMERICA

A Journalist and His Times

Bill Moyers

EDITED BY JULIE LEININGER PYCIOR

THE NEW PRESS

NEW YORK
LONDON

Published in the United States by The New Press, New York, 2004
Distributed by W. W. Norton & Company, Inc., New York

ISBN 1-56584-892-6
CIP data available

The New Press was established in 1990 as a not-for-profit alternative to the large,
commercial publishing houses currently dominating the book publishing industry.
The New Press operates in the public interest rather than for private gain,
and is committed to publishing, in innovative ways, works of educational,
cultural, and community value that are often deemed insufficiently profitable.

The New Press
38 Greene Street, 4th floor
New York, NY 10013
www.thenewpress.com

In the United Kingdom:
6 Salem Road
London W2 4BU

Composition by dix!

Printed in the United States of America

2 4 6 8 10 9 7 5 3 1

For Bob and Ford Schumann

. . . par nobile fratum . . .

Two of democracy's best friends

Contents

CONTENTS

Foreword

We journalists write on the sand and speak into the wind, and usually by the morning after there isn't a trace of what we wrote or said. The Internet has speeded up both the dissemination and the disappearance of the noise we add to the day's chatter. Millions may invite us into their living rooms, may nod in agreement or rage at our impudence, may clip our columns and stuff them in a drawer or spin them forward to distant parties via the Internet. But the moment comes when, like ice, we melt into the milieu. We're lucky if someday a grandchild, or graduate student, is curious about what we once said or wrote.

I was pleased, then, when André Schiffrin, the director of The New Press, suggested this compilation. Few things flatter a broadcast journalist more than the prospect of even the briefest half-life between hard covers. Any visit to a remainder table at the bookstore will reveal just how fleeting that half-life can be, but I found irresistible, nonetheless, the offer to make a contribution—however modest—to the world of books.

Because we are at the mercy of events, the work of journalists is as eclectic as it is transient. The world arrives at a dizzying pace; one never knows what the morning will bring, or even the next hour, and we are never sure where the trail will lead. We focus on this moving dot or that one, but we rarely pause to connect them. Reviewing these pages, I realize how much I have been guided—perhaps without even being aware of it—by the desire to try to connect some of the dots: between past and present, cause and effect, us and them, you and me. Gilbert McAllister may have been responsible for this bent. "Dr. Mac" taught the introductory anthropology course at the University of Texas. I remember to this day his opening lecture, when he recounted the years he had spent among the Apaches as a young graduate student. They had taught him the meaning of reciprocity. In the Apache tongue, he said, the word for grandfather is the same as the word for grandson; generations are linked to one another in an embrace of mutual obligation. With that he was off, expounding on his conviction that through the ages human beings have advanced more through collaboration than competition. For all the chest thumping about rugged individuals and self-made men, an ethic of cooperation inspired the social compromise that we, in our best moments, wove into a common enterprise.

My father, drawing on his own experience, understood this. As you will read in one of these selections, in his later years he often reminisced about his days as a boy growing up on the Red River, between Oklahoma and Texas. He was fourteen when his own father died during the flu epidemic in 1918. Neighbors washed my grandfather's body, neighbors dug his grave, and neighbors laid him in the earth. Through the years my father was one of several men in the church who took turns sitting beside the corpse of a departed friend or fellow congregant. He often drew the midnight shift and would go directly from his vigil to his job. Shortly before his own death, as we sat talking on the front porch, I asked him, "Why did you sit up all night when you had to drive your truck all the next day?" Without hesitation he said: "Because it was the thing we did."

The thing *we* did.

During my freshman year in college I often hitchhiked between campus and home. The route had once been Old County Line Road, down which settlers had moved into northeast Texas in the mid-eighteenth century. Historical markers now dot the way. One of them, at the spot where I used to wait for passing cars, my thumb held high, records that a John McGarrah brought his family to Texas in 1842 and nearby founded the town of Buckner. Soon a church was built, then a school, followed by a trading post. Four years later, on the Fourth of July, 1846, he and his neighbors elected their first public officials and, as part of their celebration, opened a post office. One can see there the rough progression of a social order, as well as the embryonic democratic impulse: first the prime family unit, then the wagon train, then the school for learning and the church for worship, a trading post for the goods of survival and comfort, followed by a local government for roads and public order, a communications center for contact with the larger world, and, finally, a public holiday for recreation and the celebration of common interests. A pioneering leader of the American Ethical Union, Edward L. Ericson, whose essays have informed my own journey, once described society as a web of cooperation joining individuals to family, friends, communities, and country, creating in the individual a sense of reliance on the whole, producing the "habits of the heart," in Robert Bellah's term, that are the bedrock of our social contract.

At commencement exercises I wonder if a stranger from one generation can say much that is helpful to members of a generation who are poised on a different doorstep of time. They listen, however, when I put a loaf of bread on the lectern and tell them it represents one of the most important lessons I have learned over a long life in journalism. Bread is the great reinforcer of the reality principle—that life is a social, not a solitary, endeavor. We depend for our bread on a host of others, most of them strangers, from the farmer to the baker to the deliveryman to the shopkeeper. The Lord's Prayer, so familiar and urgent to my parents during the Great Depression, invokes the first person plural, not the first person singular: "Give *us* this day our daily bread." Ericson, among others, insists that social cooperation provided the resilient environment in which American enterprise flourished. Sure, the record is stained by cruelty, racism, and violence; dedicated to the proposition that all men are created equal, Americans dispossessed the Indian and nurtured slavery in the cradle of liberty. Those settlers who poured into northeast Texas could be a violent lot; the natives they encountered became the loathsome "red man" and one in four farmers who arrived slaveless wound up owning other human beings as chattel. The social contract extended only so far. Nonetheless, over time, in the making of America individual initiative succeeded only when it led to strong systems of mutual support and we learned to move, in Ericson's description, beyond the laissez-faire philosophy of "live and let live" to an active commitment of "live and help live." Civilization, as we are constantly informed by the news of the day, is not a natural act; it is, rather, a veneer of civility stretched across primal human appetites.

Like democracy, civilization has to be willed and practiced. Otherwise, society is a war of all against all, powered by individual cunning in the pursuit of wealth and power. Look around, if you would, to see what I mean. The web of cooperation is under siege, and in these pages I try to identify the most worrisome of the indicators: economic and political elites have created islands of gilded affluence surrounded by moats of inequality wider than any since 1929; a reactionary coalition has determined to dismantle the social safety net by bankrupting the federal treasury; I believe this unraveling of the social fabric through the growing corruption of politics by money and ideology threatens the very soul of our democracy. Arguably one of the most important stories of our time is the "arms race"—waged for money instead of missiles—between the two major parties, and the indifference shown this madness by a mainstream press that emphasizes celebrity and sensationalism, speed over accuracy, and polemics over reporting. Meanwhile, a handful of media moguls with their eyes on the bottom line, which measures Americans only as consumers and not as citizens, gain more control over what we see, read, and hear.

One of my greatest rewards as a journalist derives from spotlighting citizen patriots who are still fighting for democracy against the odds, and in these pages you will meet some of them. Doris Haddock of New Hampshire, for one. Approaching the age of ninety, "Granny D" walked across the entire width of this land to protest the betrayal of democracy. I also am inspired by reformers of generations past, including journalists. As a much younger man I was moved by the biography of the Republican editor William Allen White, whose words resonate anew today. Explaining the rise of the progressive movement, he wrote,

> Into the hearts of the dominant middle class of this country had come a sense that their civilization needed recasting, that their government had fallen into the hands of self-seekers, that a new relationship should be established between the haves and the have-nots.

On the spectrum between the reformist William Allen White and the activist Granny D. you will find the bias that informs my journalism. You will not find in these pages any single system of thought, any unitary theme—only an obsession with the democratic process and gratitude for life as a continuing course in adult education.

Much of what you will read between these covers began with a speech. Mostly we journalists report and explain what others are thinking and doing; rarely do we bother to explain ourselves. Nor in our "official" work is there space, time, or justification to include extraneous personal thoughts. In my field of broadcast journalism there is virtue in the economy of words, and one is always aware of the ticking clock. A public speech offers a more intimate challenge, a more immediate test. You can look an audience in the eye, weigh the expectations or sense the indifference, single out a doubting Thomas, connect to the kindred spirit, and—if the alchemy works—experience the metamorphosis of myriad strangers into one body. There are few epiphanies to equal it. The printed page offers its own possibilities—especially the potential for intimate, thoughtful communion with the reader—and I welcome this chance to connect to new people—people who have never seen one of my television specials or been in the audience when I spoke.

Through the years many colleagues have contributed significantly to my journalism. There are too many to recall here, but in particular I want to express my appreciation to those who have served as prime researchers and editorial associates for the work reflected in this book: Rob Addy, Eric Alterman, Alex Banker, Sandra Brawarski, Elizabeth Karnes, Chris Roberts, Mike Smith, Andie Tucher, and Rebecca Wharton. To my longtime colleague, the historian Bernard Wiesberger, I owe special thanks for serving as my private tutor on one project after another, from our PBS series *A Walk Through the Twentieth Century,* to my current passion for the progressive story of America. My wife and business and creative partner, Judith Davidson Moyers, a journalist in her own right, has been a singular influence in the worldview that informs our television productions, this book, and our life together. Almost every word here passed at one time or another through the word processor of my long-time assistant, Friema Hope Norkin. For the compilation and editing of this book, as well as the encouragement to do it in the first place, I am indebted to the historian—and my friend—Julie Leininger Pycior.

Editor's Note

Julie Leininger Pycior

This book breaks new ground as the first-ever collection of Bill Moyers' speeches and commentaries. As originally spoken, these words had special resonance, from the electricity of a live speech to the intimate yet wide-ranging effect of a television commentary. At the same time the written version of a spoken piece can resonate with a power of its own, particularly when the words are good ones. Bill Moyers carefully crafts the commentaries and speeches that he delivers aloud, and when some of these transcripts have appeared on the Internet, the words have proven to be a sensation. I lost count of the people who mentioned having read online one of his most recent speeches. "This Is Your Story. Pass It On."—all of them eager to express their enthusiasm, even gratitude for the words they read. Now it and many other evocative pieces are here, together in one place, portable and permanent.

The editing consisted of converting speeches and commentaries into essay form: mostly straightforward modifications such as deleting references to a live audience. Then Bill Moyers reworded and/or recast portions of his original prose. A note about the date at the end of each selection: the year is given (in the case of the program essays, the month and year), but not the exact day, reflecting the fact that each selection has been modified at least in part from its form as originally spoken.

André Schiffrin, director of The New Press, suggested this project and provided invaluable support and advice. In fact, one of the many joys of collecting these pieces has been the privilege of working with such a dedicated champion of worthwhile publishing. I am grateful as well to New Press politics editor Andy Hsiao for his sage counsel and to Jonathan Shainin, late of The New Press, who helped keep us connected. At Public Affairs Television (PAT), Judith and Bill Moyers head a group of exceptionally dedicated people. Friema Hope Norkin quickly came up with the electronic versions of the original speeches and provided cheerful, able assistance at every point in the process. Archivist Doris Lang Thomas showed keen interest in the project from the start, made valuable content suggestions, and located thirty-year-old commentaries with dispatch. Her colleagues Marsha Sorotick and Patricia Whalen also contributed valuably to this endeavor. Other helpful PATers included Diana Warner, Ismael González, and Lisa Kalikow. I am grateful as always to Stan Pycior, my rock, and above all to Bill Moyers. It is a great privilege to work with this giant of broadcast journalism, a fact that was brought home to me constantly. In the middle of my work—even with mundane tasks—the words themselves kept shedding light on my own life's journey.

MOYERS ON AMERICA

Part One

AMERICA NOW

THIS IS YOUR STORY. PASS IT ON.

On my sixteenth birthday in 1950 I went to work for the daily newspaper in the small East Texas town where I grew up. It was a good place to be a cub reporter—small enough to navigate but big enough to keep me busy and learning something every day. I soon had a stroke of luck. Some of the old-timers were on vacation or out sick, and I got assigned to cover what came to be known as the "Housewives' Rebellion." Fifteen women in my hometown decided not to pay the Social Security withholding tax for their domestic workers. They argued that Social Security was unconstitutional, that imposing it was taxation without representation, and that—here's my favorite part—"requiring us to collect [the tax] is no different from requiring us to collect the garbage." They hired themselves a lawyer—none other than Martin Dies Jr., the former congressman best known, or worst known, for his work as head of the House Committee on Un-American Activities in the 1930s and 1940s. He was no more effective at defending rebellious women than he had been protecting against communist subversives, and eventually the housewives wound up holding their noses and paying the tax.

The stories I wrote for my local paper were picked up by the Associated Press wire. One day the managing editor called me over and pointed to the AP ticker beside his desk. Moving across the wire was a notice citing one Bill Moyers and the paper for the reporting we had done on the "rebellion."

That hooked me, and in one way or another—after a detour through seminary and then into politics and government for a spell—I've been covering the class war ever since. Those women in Marshall, Texas, were its advance guard. Not bad people, they were regulars at church; their children were my friends, many of them were active in community affairs, and their husbands were pillars of the business and professional class in town. They were respectable and upstanding citizens all, so it took me a while to figure out what had brought on that spasm of reactionary rebellion. It came to me one day, much later. They simply couldn't see beyond their own prerogatives. Fiercely loyal to their families, to their clubs, charities, and congregations—fiercely loyal, in other words, to their own kind—they narrowly defined membership in democracy to include only people like them. The women who washed and ironed their laundry, wiped their children's bottoms, made their husbands' beds, and cooked their families' meals— these women, too, would grow old and frail, sick and decrepit, lose their husbands and face the ravages of time alone, with nothing to show from their years of labor but the creases in their brow and the knots on their knuckles. So be it; even on the distaff side of laissez-faire, security was personal, not social, and what injustice existed this side of heaven would no doubt be redeemed beyond the pearly gates. God would surely be just to the poor once they got past Judgment Day.

In one way or another, this is the oldest story in America: the struggle to determine whether "we, the people" is a spiritual idea embedded in a political reality—one nation, indivisible—or merely a charade masquerading as piety and manipulated by the powerful and privileged to sustain their own way of life at the expense of others.

I should make it clear that I don't harbor any idealized notion of politics and democracy; after all, I worked for Lyndon Johnson. Nor do I romanticize "the people." You should read my mail or listen to the vitriol virtually spat at my answering machine. I understand what the politician meant who said of the Texas House of Representatives, "If you think these guys are bad, you should see their constituents."

But there is nothing idealized or romantic about the difference between a society whose arrangements roughly serve all its citizens and one whose institutions have been converted into a stupendous fraud. That difference can be the difference between democracy and oligarchy.

Look at our history. The American Revolution ushered in what one historian called "the age of democratic revolutions." For the Great Seal of the United States the new Congress went all the way back to the Roman poet Virgil: *novus ordo seclorum,* "a new age now begins." Page Smith reminds us that "their ambition was not merely to free themselves from dependence and subordination to the Crown but to inspire people everywhere to create agencies of government and forms of common social life that would offer greater dignity and hope to the exploited and suppressed"—to those, in other words, who had been the losers. Not surprisingly, the winners often resisted. In the early years of constitution making in the states and the emerging nation, aristocrats wanted a government of propertied "gentlemen" to keep the scales tilted in their favor. Battling on the other side were moderates and even those radicals harboring the extraordinary idea of letting all white males have the vote. Luckily, the weapons were words and ideas, not bullets. Through compromise and conciliation the draftsmen achieved a constitution of checks and balances that is now the oldest in the world, even as the revolution of democracy that inspired it remains a tempestuous adolescent whose destiny is still up for grabs. For all the rhetoric about "life, liberty, and the pursuit of happiness," it took a civil war to free the slaves and another hundred years to invest their freedom with meaning. Women gained the right to vote only in my mother's time. New ages don't arrive overnight, or without blood, sweat, and tears.

In this regard we are heirs of a great movement, the Progressive movement, which began late in the nineteenth century and re-made the American experience piece by piece until it peaked in the last third of the twentieth century. (I call it the Progressive movement for lack of a more precise term.) Its aim was to keep blood pumping through the veins of democracy when others were ready to call in the mortician. Progressives exalted and ex-tended the original American revolution. They spelled out new terms of partnership between the people and their rulers. And they kindled a flame that lit some of the most prosperous decades in modern history, not only here but in aspiring democracies everywhere, especially those of Western Europe.

Step back with me to the curtain-raiser, the founding conven-tion of the People's Party—better known as the Populists—in 1892. Mainly cotton and wheat farmers from the recently recon-structed South and the newly settled Great Plains, they had come on hard, hard times, driven to the wall by falling prices for their crops on one hand and by racking interest rates, freight charges, and supply costs, on the other: all this in the midst of a booming and growing industrial America. They were angry, and their plat-form—issued deliberately on the Fourth of July—pulled no punches. "We meet," it said, "in the midst of a nation brought to the verge of moral, political and material ruin. . . . Corruption dominates the ballot box, the [state] legislatures and the Congress and touches even the bench. . . . The newspapers are largely subsidized or muzzled, public opinion silenced. . . . The fruits of the toil of millions are boldly stolen to build up colossal fortunes for a few."

Furious words indeed from rural men and women who were traditionally conservative and whose memories of taming the frontier were fresh and personal, but who in their fury invoked an American tradition as powerful as frontier individualism, namely, the war on inequality—especially government's role in promoting and preserving inequality by favoring the rich. The Founding Fathers turned their backs on the idea of property qualifications for holding office under the Constitution because they wanted absolutely no "veneration for wealth" in the document. Thomas Jefferson, while claiming no interest in politics, built up a Democratic-Republican party to take the government back from the speculators and "stock-jobbers" who were in the saddle in 1800. Andrew Jackson slew the monster Second Bank of the United States, the six-hundred-pound gorilla of the credit system in the 1830s, in the name of the people versus the aristocrats who sat on the bank's governing board.

All these leaders were on record in favor of small government, but their opposition wasn't simply to government as such. They objected to government's power to confer *privilege* on the democracy's equivalent of the royal favorites of monarchist days: on the rich, on the insiders, on what today we know as the crony capitalists. The Populists knew it was the government that granted millions of acres of public land to the railroad builders. It was the government that gave the manufacturers of farm machinery a monopoly of the domestic market by a protective tariff that was no longer necessary to shelter infant industries. It was the government that contracted the national currency and sparked a deflationary cycle that crushed debtors and fattened the wallets of creditors. And those who made the great fortunes used them to buy the legislative and judicial favors that kept them on top. So the Populists recognized one great principle: the job of preserving equality of opportunity and democracy demanded the end of any unholy alliance between government and wealth. It was, to quote that platform again, "from the same womb of *governmental injustice*" that tramps and millionaires were bred (emphasis added).

The question remained, however: how was the democratic revolution to be revived, the promise of the Declaration reclaimed? How were Americans to restore government to its job of promoting the *general* welfare? And here the Populists made a breakthrough to another principle. In a modern, large-scale, industrial, and nationalized economy it wasn't enough simply to curb the government's outreach. Such a policy would simply leave power in the hands of the great corporations whose existence was inseparable from growth and progress. The answer was to turn government into an active player in the economy, at the very least enforcing fair play and when necessary being the friend, the helper, and the agent of the people at large in the contest against entrenched power. As a result, the Populist platform called for government loans to farmers about to lose their mortgaged homesteads, for government granaries to grade and store their crops fairly, for governmental inflation of the currency (a classical plea of debtors), and for some decidedly nonclassical actions: government ownership of the railroad, telephone, and telegraph systems; a graduated (i.e., progressive) tax on incomes; a flat ban on subsidies to "any private corporation." Moreover, in order to ensure that the government stayed on the side of the people, the party called for two electoral reforms, the initiative and referendum and the direct election of senators.

Predictably, the Populists were denounced, feared, and mocked

as fanatical hayseeds ignorantly playing with socialist fire. They received twenty-two electoral votes for their 1892 candidate, plus
some congressional seats and state houses, but this would prove to
be the party's peak. America wasn't—and probably still isn't—
ready for a new major party. The People's Party was a spent rocket
by 1904. At the same time, when political organizations perish,
their key ideas endure, and this is a perspective of great importance to today's progressives. Much of the Populist agenda would
become law within a few years of the party's extinction because
their goals were generally shared by a rising generation of young
Republicans and Democrats who, justly or not, were seen as less
outrageously outdated than the embattled farmers. These were
the Progressives, the intellectual forebears of those of us who
today call ourselves by the same name.

They were a diverse lot, held together by a common admiration
of progress—hence the name—and a shared dismay at the paradox of poverty stubbornly persisting in the midst of progress like
an unwanted guest at a wedding. Of course they welcomed, just as
we do, the new marvels in the gift bag of technology—the telephones, the automobiles, the electrically powered urban transport
and lighting systems, the indoor heating and plumbing, the
processed foods and home appliances and machine-made clothing that reduced the sweat and drudgery of homemaking and
were affordable to an ever-swelling number of people. At the same
time, however, they saw the underside: the slums lurking in the
shadows of the glittering cities; the exploited and unprotected
workers whose low-paid labor filled the horn of plenty for others;
the misery of those whom age, sickness, accident, or hard times
condemned to servitude and poverty with no hope of comfort or
security.

Incredibly, in little more than a century, the still-young revolution of 1776 was being strangled by the hard grip of a merciless ruling class. The large corporations that were called into being by modern industrialism after 1865—the end of the Civil War—had combined into trusts capable of making minions of both politics and government. What Henry George called "an immense wedge" was being forced through American society by "the maldistribution of wealth, status, and opportunity."

We should pause here to consider that this is Karl Rove's cherished period of American history; it was, as I read him, the seminal influence on the man who is said to be the mastermind of George W. Bush's success. From his own public comments and my reading of the record, it is apparent that Karl Rove has modeled the Bush presidency on that of William McKinley, who was in the White House from 1897 to 1901, and modeled himself on Mark Hanna, the man who virtually manufactured McKinley. Hanna had one consummate passion: to serve corporate and imperial power. He believed without compunction, according to a critic, that "the state of Ohio existed for property. It had no other function. . . . Great wealth was to be gained through monopoly, through using the State for private ends; it was axiomatic therefore that businessmen should run the government and run it for personal profit."

Mark Hanna made William McKinley governor of Ohio by shaking down the corporate interests of the day. Fortunately, it was said, McKinley had the invaluable gift of emitting sonorous platitudes as though they were recently discovered truth. Behind his benign gaze the wily intrigues of Mark Hanna saw to it that first Ohio and then Washington were, in his words, "ruled by business . . . by bankers, railroads, and public utility corporations." Any who opposed the oligarchy were smeared as disturbers of the peace, socialists, anarchists, or worse. Back then they didn't bother with hollow euphemisms such as "compassionate conservatism" to disguise the raw reactionary politics that produced government of, by, and for the ruling corporate class. They just saw the loot and went for it.

The historian Clinton Rossiter describes this as the period of "the great train robbery of American intellectual history." Conservatives—or, better, pro-corporate apologists—hijacked the vocabulary of Jeffersonian liberalism and turned words such as *progress, opportunity,* and *individualism* into tools for making the plunder of America sound like divine right. This "degenerate and unlovely age," as one historian calls it, seemingly exists in the mind of Karl Rove as the age of inspiration for the politics and governance of America today.

It is no wonder, then, that what troubled our Progressive forebears was not only the miasma of poverty in their nostrils but also the sour stink of a political system for sale. The United States Senate was a millionaires' club. Money given to the political machines that controlled nominations could buy controlling influence in city halls, statehouses, and even courtrooms. Reforms and improvements ran into the immovable resistance of the almighty dollar. What, Progressives wondered, would this would this do to the principles of popular government? All of them, whatever their political party, were inspired by the gospel of democracy. Inevitably, this swept them into the currents of politics, whether as active officeholders or persistent advocates.

Here is a small but representative sampling of their ranks. Jane Addams forsook the comforts of a well-to-do college graduate's life to live in Hull House in the midst of a disease-ridden and crowded Chicago immigrant neighborhood, determined to make it an educational and social center that would bring pride, health, and beauty into the lives of her poor neighbors. In her words, "an almost passionate devotion to the ideals of democracy" inspired

Addams to combat the prevailing notion "that the wellbeing of a privileged few might justly be built upon the ignorance and sacrifice of the many." Community and fellowship were the lessons she drew from her teachers, Jesus and Abraham Lincoln, but people simply helping one another couldn't move mountains of disadvantage. She came to see that "private beneficence" was not enough. To bring justice to the poor would take more than soup kitchens and fund-raising prayer meetings. "Social arrangements," she wrote, "can be transformed through man's conscious and deliberate effort." Take note: she spoke not of individual regeneration or the magic of the market but of conscious, cooperative effort.

Meet a couple of muckraking journalists. Jacob Riis lugged his heavy camera up and down the staircases of New York's disease-ridden, firetrap tenements to photograph the unspeakable crowding, the inadequate toilets, the starved and hollow-eyed children, and the filth on the walls so thick that his crude flash equipment sometimes set it afire. Bound between hard covers, with Riis's commentary, these images showed comfortable New Yorkers "how the other half lives." They were powerful ammunition for reformers who eventually brought an end to tenement housing by state legislation. For his part, Lincoln Steffens, college- and graduate-school-educated, left his books to learn life from the bottom up as a police-beat reporter on New York's streets. Then, as a magazine writer, he exposed the links between city bosses and businessmen that made it possible for builders and factory owners to ignore safety codes and get away with it. But the villain was neither the boodler nor the businessman. It was the indifference of a public that "deplore[d] our politics and laud[ed] our business; that transformed law, medicine, literature and religion into simply business." Steffens was out to slay the dragon of exalting "the commercial spirit" over the goals of patriotism and national prosperity. "I am not a scientist," he said. "I am a journalist. I did not gather the facts and arrange them patiently for permanent preservation and laboratory analysis. . . . My purpose was . . . to see if the shameful facts, spread out in all their shame, would not burn through our civic shamelessness and set fire to American pride."

If corrupt politics bred diseases that could be fatal to democracy, then good politics was the antidote. That was the discovery of Ray Stannard Baker, another journalistic Progressive. He started out detesting election-time catchwords and slogans, but he came to see that "politics could not be abolished or even adjourned . . . it was in its essence the method by which communities worked out their common problems. It was one of the principle arts of living peacefully in a crowded world." (Compare that to Grover Norquist's latest declaration of war on the body politic: "We are trying to change the tones in the state capitals— and turn them toward bitter nastiness and partisanship." He went on to say that bipartisanship "is another name for date rape.")

There are more, too many more to call to the witness stand here, but at the very least let us examine in brief some of the things they had to say. There were educators such as the economist John R. Commons or the sociologist Edward A. Ross, who believed that the function of social science was not simply to dissect society for nonjudgmental analysis and academic promotion but to help in finding solutions to social problems. It was Ross who pointed out that morality in a modern world had a social dimension. In *Sin and Society* (1907) he told readers that the sins "blackening the face of our time" were of a new variety, and not yet recognized as such. "The man who picks pockets with a railway rebate, murders with an adulterant instead of a bludgeon, burglarizes with a 'rake-off' instead of a jimmy, cheats with a company instead of a deck of cards, or scuttles his town instead of his ship, does not feel on his brow the brand of a malefactor." In other words, upstanding individuals could plot corporate crimes and sleep the sleep of the just without the sting of social stigma or the pangs of conscience. Like Kenneth Lay, they could even be invited into the White House to write their own regulations.

Here are just two final bits of testimony from actual politicians: first, Brand Whitlock, mayor of Toledo. He first learned his politics as a beat reporter in Chicago. One of his lessons was that "the alliance between the lobbyists and the lawyers of the great corporation interests on the one hand, and the managers of both the great political parties on the other, was a fact, the worst feature of which was that no one seemed to care." Then there is Tom Johnson, the Progressive mayor of Cleveland in the early 1900s—a businessman converted to social activism. His major battles were to impose regulation, or even municipal takeover, on the private companies that were meant to provide affordable public transportation and utilities but in fact crushed competitors, overcharged customers, secured franchises and licenses for a song, and paid virtually nothing in taxes—all through their pocketbook control of lawmakers and judges. Johnson's argument for public ownership was simple: "If you don't own them, they will own you." It's why advocates of clean elections today argue that if anybody's going to buy Congress, it should be the people. When advised that businessman got their way in Washington because they had lobbies and consumers had none, Tom Johnson responded: "If Congress were true to the principles of democracy it would be the people's lobby." What a radical contrast to the House of Representatives today!

Our political, moral, and intellectual forebears occupy a long and honorable roster. They include wonderful characters such as Dr. Alice Hamilton, a pioneer in industrially caused diseases, who spent long years clambering up and down ladders in factories and mineshafts—in long skirts—ferreting out the toxic substances that sickened workers, whom she would track right into their sickbeds to get leads and tip-offs for further investigations. There's Harvey Wiley, the chemist from Indiana who, from a bureaucrat's desk in the Department of Agriculture, relentlessly warred on foods laden with risky preservatives and adulterants with the help of his "poison squad" of young assistants who volunteered as guinea pigs. Or lawyers such as the brilliant Harvard graduate Louis Brandeis, who took on corporate attorneys defending child labor or long and harsh conditions for female workers. Brandeis argued that the state had a duty to protect the health of working women and children. Imagine that!

To be sure, these Progressives weren't saintly. Their glory years coincided with the heyday of lynching and segregation, of empire and the Big Stick and the bold theft of the Panama Canal, of immigration restriction and ethnic stereotypes. Some were themselves businessmen only hoping to control an unruly marketplace by regulation. By and large, however, they were conservative reformers. They aimed to preserve the existing balance between wealth and commonwealth. Their common enemy was unchecked privilege, their common hope was a better democracy, and their common weapon was informed public opinion.

In a few short years the Progressive spirit made possible the election not only of reform mayors and governors but of national figures such as Senator George Norris of Nebraska, Senator Robert M. La Follette of Wisconsin, and even that hard-to-classify political genius, Theodore Roosevelt, all three of them Republicans.

Here is the simplest laundry list of what was accomplished at the state and federal levels: publicly regulated or owned transportation, sanitation, and utilities system; the partial restoration of competition in the marketplace through improved antitrust laws; increased fairness in taxation; expansion of the public education and juvenile justice systems; safer workplaces and guarantees of compensation to workers injured on the job; oversight of the purity of water, medicines, and foods; conservation of the national wilderness heritage against overdevelopment; honest bidding on any public mining, lumbering, and ranching. All those safeguards were provided not by the automatic workings of free enterprise but by implementing the idea in the Declaration of Independence that the people had a right to governments that best promoted their "safety and happiness."

The mighty Progressive wave peaked in 1912, but the ideas unleashed by it forged the politics of the twentieth century. Like his cousin Theodore, Franklin Roosevelt argued that the real enemies of enlightened capitalism were "the malefactors of great wealth"—the "economic royalists"—from whom capitalism would have to be saved by reform and regulation. Progressive government became an embedded tradition of Democrats—the heart of Franklin Roosevelt's New Deal and Harry Truman's Fair Deal. Even Dwight D. Eisenhower honored this tradition; he did not want to tear down the house Progressives' ideas had built, only put it under different managers. The Progressive impulse had its final fling in the landslide of 1964, when Lyndon Johnson—a son of the west Texas hill country, where the Populist rebellion had been nurtured in the 1890s—won the public endorsement for what he meant to be the capstone in the arch of the New Deal.

I had a modest role in that era. I shared in its exhilaration and its failures. We went too far too fast, overreached at home and in Vietnam, failed to examine some assumptions, and misjudged the rising discontents and fierce backlash engendered by the passions of the time. Democrats grew so proprietary in Washington, D.C., that a corpulent, complacent political establishment couldn't recognize its own intellectual bankruptcy or see the Beltway encircling it and beginning to separate it from the working people of America. The failure of Democratic politicians and public thinkers to respond to popular discontents—to the daily lives of workers, consumers, parents, and ordinary taxpayers—allowed a resurgent conservatism to convert public concern and hostility into a crusade that masked the resurrection of social Darwinism as a moral philosophy, multinational corporations as a governing class, and the theology of markets as a transcendental belief system.

As a citizen, I don't like the consequences of this crusade, but I respect the conservatives for their successful strategy in gaining control of the national agenda. Their stated and open aim is to strip from government all its functions except those that reward their rich and privileged benefactors. They are quite candid about it, even acknowledging proudly the mean spirit invoked to accomplish their ambitions. Their leading strategist in Washington, Grover Norquist, in commenting on the fiscal crisis in the states and its effect on schools and poor people, said, "I hope one of them"—one of the states—"goes bankrupt." So much for compassionate conservatism. But at least Norquist says what he means and means what he says. The White House pursues the same homicidal dream without saying so. Instead of shrinking the government, they're filling the bathtub with so much debt that it floods the house, waterlogs the economy, and washes away services that for decades have lifted millions of Americans out of destitution and into the middle class. And what happens once the public's property has been flooded? Privatize it. Sell it at a discounted rate to their corporate cronies.

It is the most radical assault on the notion of one nation, indivisible, that has occurred in our lifetime. I simply don't understand it—or the malice in which it is steeped. Many people are nostalgic for a golden age; these people seem to long for the Gilded Age.

That I can grasp. They measure America only by how it serves their own kind, like Marshall housewives, and they bask in the company of the new corporate aristocracy, as privileged a class as we have seen since the plantation owners of antebellum America and the court of Louis XIV. What I can't explain is the rage of these counterrevolutionaries to dismantle every last brick of the social contract. At this advanced age I accept the fact that the tension between haves and have-nots is built into human psychology and society itself—it's ever with us. However, I'm just as puzzled as to why, with right-wing wrecking crews blasting away at social benefits once considered invulnerable, Democrats are fearful of being branded "class warriors" in a war the other side started and is determined to win. I don't get why conceding your opponent's premises and fighting on his turf isn't a surefire prescription for irrelevance and ultimately obsolescence. But I confess as well that I don't know how to resolve the social issues that have driven wedges into the ranks of the working- and lower-middle-classes and divided them from the more affluent, upper-middle-class professionals and highly educated who were once their allies. Nor do I know how to reconfigure Progressive politics to fit into an age of sound bites and polling dominated by a media oligarchy whose corporate journalists are neutered and whose right-wing publicists have no shame.

What I do know is this: while the social dislocations and meanness that galvanized Progressives in the nineteenth century are resurgent, so is the vision of justice, fairness, and equality. No challenge to America is greater than to open suffrage and the marketplace to new and marginal people—and this is the Progressive vision. It's a powerful vision if only there are people around to fight for it. The battle to renew democracy has enormous resources to call upon—and great precedents for inspiration. Consider the experience of James Bryce, who published *The Great Commonwealth* back in 1895, at the height of the first Gilded Age. Americans, Bryce said, "were hopeful and philanthropic." He saw firsthand the ills of that "dark and unlovely age," but he went on to say, "a hundred times I have been disheartened by the facts I was stating: a hundred times has the recollection of the abounding strength and vitality of the nation chased away those tremors."

What will it take to get back in the fight? The first order of business is to understand the real interests and deep opinions of the American people. What are these?

- That a Social Security card is not a private portfolio statement but a membership ticket in a society where we all contribute to a common treasury so that none need face the indignities of poverty in old age
- That tax evasion is not a form of conserving investment capital but a brazen abandonment of responsibility to the country
- That income inequality is not a sign of freedom of opportunity at work, because if it persists and grows, then unless you believe that some people are naturally born to ride and some to wear saddles, it's a sign that opportunity is less than equal
- That self-interest is a great motivator for production and progress but is amoral unless contained within the framework of social justice
- That the rich have the right to buy more cars than anyone else, more homes, vacations, gadgets, and gizmos, but they do not have the right to buy more democracy than anyone else
- That public services, when privatized, serve only those who can afford them and weaken the sense that we all rise and fall together as "one nation, indivisible"

- That concentration in the production of goods may sometimes be useful and efficient, but monopoly over the dissemination of ideas is tyranny
- That prosperity requires good wages and benefits for workers
- That our nation can no more survive as half democracy and half oligarchy than it could survive half slave and half free, and that keeping it from becoming all oligarchy is steady work—our work

Ideas have power—as long as they are not frozen in doctrine—but they need legs. The eight-hour day; the minimum wage; the conservation of natural resources and the protection of our air, water, and land; women's rights and civil rights; free trade unions; Social Security; a civil service based on merit—all these were launched as citizens' movements and won the endorsement of the political class only after long struggles and in the face of bitter opposition and sneering attacks. Democracy doesn't work without citizen activism and participation. Trickle-down politics is no more effective than trickle-down economics. Moreover, civilization happens because we don't leave things to other people. What's right and good doesn't come naturally. You have to stand up and fight as if the cause depends on you. Allow yourself that conceit—to believe that the flame of democracy will never go out as long as there's one candle in one citizen's hand.

"Democracy is not a lie," wrote Henry Demarest Lloyd, the Progressive journalist whose book *Wealth Against Commonwealth* laid open the Standard Oil trust a century ago. Lloyd came to the conclusion that to

regenerate the individual is a half truth. The reorganization of the society which he makes and which makes him is the other part. The love of liberty *became* liberty in America by clothing itself in the complicated group of strengths known as the government of the United States. Democracy is not a lie. There live[s] in the body of the commonality unexhausted virtue and the ever-refreshed strength which can rise equal to any problems of progress. In the hope of tapping some reserve of their power of self-help, this story is told to the people.

This is our story, the Progressive story of America. Pass it on.

—2003

WHICH AMERICA
WILL WE BE NOW?

For years now I've been taking every possible opportunity to talk about the soul of democracy. "Something is deeply wrong with politics today," I told anyone who would listen. I wasn't referring to the partisan mudslinging, the negative TV ads, the excessive polling, or the empty campaigns. I was talking about something more fundamental, something troubling at the core of politics. The soul of democracy—the essence of the word itself— is government of, by, and for the people, and the soul of democracy has been dying, drowning in a rising tide of big money contributed by a narrow, unrepresentative elite that has betrayed the faith of citizens in self-government.

What happened immediately after the September 11 attacks would seem to put the lie to my fears. Americans rallied together in a way that I cannot remember since World War II. The terrorist atrocity reminded us of a basic truth at the heart of our democracy: No matter our wealth or status or faith, we are all equal before the law, in the voting booth, and when death rains down from the sky.

We have also been reminded that despite years of scandals and political corruption, despite the stream of stories of personal greed and Gucci-clad pirates scamming the Treasury, despite the retreat from the public sphere and the turn toward private privilege, despite squalor for the poor and gated communities for the rich, the great mass of Americans had not given up on the idea of "we, the people." They had refused to accept the notion, promoted so diligently by our friends at the right-wing foundations, that government should be shrunk to a size where, as Grover Norquist infamously put it, they can drown it in a bathtub.

These right-wing ideologues, by the way, teamed up with deep-pocket bankers—many from Texas, with ties to the Bush White House—to stop America from cracking down on terrorist money havens even after September 11. Better that terrorists get their dirty money than tax cheaters be prevented from hiding theirs. These are the very people we have seen wrap themselves in the flag and sing "The Star-Spangled Banner" with gusto, even as they are attempting to exempt their wealthy benefactors from bearing a fair share of the cost of the government that must fight the war on terrorism.

Contrary to the right-wing denigration of government, however, the heroes of the hour were public servants. I mean those brave firefighters and policemen and Port Authority workers and emergency rescue personnel who sprang into action on September 11—public employees all, most of them drawing a modest middle-class income for extremely dangerous work. They caught our imaginations not only for their heroic deeds but because we know so many people like them, people we took for granted. For once, our TV screens were filled with the modest declarations of average Americans coming to each other's aid. For once, we could imagine a new beginning, a renewal of civic values that might leave our society stronger in the pursuit of the commonwealth.

For a season, in the wake of September 11, there was a change in how Americans view their government. For the first time in more than thirty years a majority of people said they trusted the federal government to do the right thing at least "most of the time." It's as if the clock has been rolled back to the early 1960s, before Vietnam and Watergate took such a toll on the gross national psychology. This newfound respect for public service—this faith in public collaboration was based in part on how people viewed what we have done collectively in response to the attacks. To most Americans, government no longer meant a faceless bureaucrat or a cynical politician auctioning access to the highest bidder. It meant a courageous rescuer or selfless soldier. Instead of our political representatives spending their evenings clinking glasses with fat cats, they were out walking among the wounded. For once, they seemed part of us.

Alas, it didn't take long for the wartime opportunists—the mercenaries of Washington, the lobbyists, lawyers, and political fundraisers—to crawl out of their offices on K Street determined to grab what they can for their clients. While in New York we were still attending memorial services for firemen and police, while everywhere Americans' cheeks were still stained with tears, while the president called for patriotism, prayers, and piety, the predators of Washington were up to their old tricks in the pursuit of private plunder at public expense. In the wake of this awful tragedy wrought by terrorism, they were cashing in. What is the memorial they would offer the thousands of people who died in the attacks? The legacy they would leave the children who lost a parent in the horror? How do they propose to fight the long and costly war on terrorism America now had to undertake? Why, restore the three-martini lunch—that will surely strike fear in the heart of Osama bin Laden. I'm not making this up; bringing back the deductible lunch was one of the proposals that surfaced post 9/11. And cut capital gains for the wealthy, naturally—that's our patriotic duty, too. While we're at it, eliminate the corporate alternative minimum tax, enacted fifteen years ago to prevent corpora-

One Year Later

My colleague was in the subway below the World Trade Center
when the first plane hit at 8:46 on September 11 a year ago.
Walking up the stairs to the street just as the second plane hit, she
heard the boom, glanced toward the flaming towers, saw falling
bodies, and shuddered. A wave of heat descended on her, and she
ran, reaching safety before the buildings came down. For two
months she sat at the window of her apartment, paralyzed by
fear. The sound of a plane would take her back to that morning,
as if she had witnessed the beginning of the world coming to an
end. A year later she still has nightmares, still sees, in the poet's
prophetic metaphor, "the great dark birds of history" that
plunged into our lives.

She's not alone. All of us now live at Ground Zero. Sitting at
our window, we wonder what's next; we walk looking over our
shoulder apprehensively. This is what terrorists want, of course.
They aim to pillage our peace of mind, deprive us of trust and
confidence, possess our psyche, and keep us from ever again believing in a safe, decent, or just world and from working to bring
it about. This is their real target: to turn each and every imagination into a personal Afghanistan, a private hell, where they can
rule by fear, as the Taliban did.

They win only if we let them, only if we become like them:
vengeful, imperious, intolerant, paranoid, invoking a God of
wrath. Having lost faith in themselves, zealots have nothing left
but a holy cause. They win if we become holy warriors, too: if in
trying to save democracy, we destroy it; if we strike first, murder-
ing innocent people as they did; if we show contempt for how
others see us, exploit patriotism to increase privilege, confuse
power with the law and secrecy with security; and if we permit
our leaders to use our fear of terrorism to make us afraid of the
truth.

What, then, can I say to my colleague, to myself, to all of us
survivors tempted to sit there in the chair by the window? Just

this: we are vulnerable not only to the fear of them but to our own shaken faith in ourselves. I keep reminding myself to remember not only the terror but the beauty revealed that day, when through the smoke and fire we glimpsed the heroism, compassion, and sacrifice of ordinary people who did the best of things in the worst of times. I keep telling myself that this beauty in us is real. It makes democracy possible, and no terrorist can take it from us. Remembering this, one year later, we can praise the mutilated world and get on with our work. Democracy is our work, and there is much to do if we are to keep it.

—*September 2002*

tions from taking so many credits and deductions that they owed little if any taxes. But don't just repeal their minimum tax; refund to those corporations all the minimum tax they have ever been assessed.

What else could America do to strike at the terrorists? Why, slip in a special tax break for poor General Electric. Don't worry about NBC, CNBC, or MSNBC reporting it; they're all in the GE family. It's time for Churchillian courage, we were told. So how would this crowd ensure that future generations will look back and say, "This was their finest hour", Easy. Give coal producers more freedom to pollute. Shovel generous tax breaks to giant energy companies. Open the Alaskan wilderness to drilling—that's something to remember the eleventh of September for. And while the red, white, and blue waves at half-mast over the land of the free and the home of the brave, why, give the president the power to discard democratic debate and the rule of law concerning controversial trade agreements, and set up secret tribunals to run roughshod over local communities trying to protect their environment and health. If I sound a little bitter about this, I am; the president rightly appeals every day for sacrifice. But to these mercenaries sacrifice is for suckers. I am bitter, yes, and sad. Our business and political elites owe us better than this. After all, it was they who declared class war twenty years ago, and it was they who won. They're on top. If ever they were going to put patriotism over profits, if ever they were going to practice the magnanimity of winners, this was the moment. To hide behind the flag while ripping off a country in crisis fatally separates them from the common course of American life.

When Dick Armey, the Republican majority leader in the House, said "it wouldn't be commensurate with the American spirit" to provide unemployment and other benefits to laid-off airline workers, once again the Republican party was living down to Harry Truman's description of the GOP as "guardians of privilege." As for Truman's Democratic party—the party of the New Deal and the Fair Deal—well, there was the Democratic National Committee, post 9-11, using the terrorist attacks to call for widening the soft-money loophole in our election laws. H.L. Mencken got it right when he said, "Whenever you hear a man speak of his love for his country, it is a sign that he expects to be paid for it."

Let's face it: these realities present citizens with no options but to climb back in the ring. We are in what educators call "a teachable moment." What's at stake—need I say it?—is the soul of democracy. Democracy wasn't canceled on September 11, but democracy won't survive if citizens turn into lemmings. Yes, the president is our commander in chief, but we are not the president's subjects. While firemen and police were racing into the fires of hell in downtown New York, and while our soldiers and airmen and marines were putting their lives on the line in Afghanistan, the administration and its congressional allies were

War Is War

Iraq is not Vietnam, but war is war. Some may recall that I was press secretary to Lyndon Johnson during the escalation of war in Vietnam. Like the White House today, we didn't talk very much about what the war would cost. In the beginning we weren't sure, and we didn't really want to know too soon, anyway. We were afraid of what telling Congress and the public the true cost of the war would do to the rest of the budget: the money for education, poverty, Medicare. In time, however, we had to figure it out and come clean.

It wasn't the price tag that hurt as much as it was the body count. The dead were coming back in such numbers that LBJ grew morose, and sometimes took to bed with the covers pulled above his eyes, as if he could avoid the ghosts of young men marching around in his head. I thought of this the other day, when President Bush spoke of the loss of American lives in Iraq. He said, "I'm the one who will have to look the mothers in the eye." LBJ said almost the same thing. No president can help but think of the mothers, widows, and orphans. The fathers, too; their hearts can break from grief.

Mr. Bush is amassing a mighty American armada in the Middle East: incredible firepower. Surely he knows that even a "clean" war—a war fought with laser beams, long-range missiles, high-flying bombers, and remote controls—gets down and dirty, especially for the other side. We forget there are mothers and fathers on the other side. I've often wondered about the parents of Vietnamese children burned by our napalm, or of Afghan children smashed and broken by our bombs. On the *NBC Nightly News* one evening I saw a report from Afghanistan with aerial photography of little white lights: heat images of people on foot about to be attacked as they fled a mosque. Were they al-Qaeda or just the faithful at worship? We'll never know, but their kin do, and so will the mothers and fathers in Iraq. Saddam won't mind the losses, even if he escapes. The death of his own people seems never to perturb the man. As for us, well, the spoils of victory include amnesia.

Ah, the seduction of war: the adrenaline that flows to men behind desks at the very thought of the armies that will march, the missiles that will fly, the ships that will sail on their command. Our secretary of defense has a plaque on his desk that reads, "Aggressive fighting for the right is the noblest sport the world affords." I don't think so. War may sometimes be a necessity; to treat it as sport is obscene. To launch an armada against Hussein's own hostage population, a people who have not fired a shot at us in anger, seems a crude and poor alternative to shrewd, disciplined diplomacy and the forging of a true alliance acting in the name of international law.

Don't get me wrong. Vietnam didn't make me a dove; it made me read the Constitution. Government's first obligation is to defend its citizens. There's nothing in the Constitution that says it's permissible for a great nation to launch a preemptive attack against a captive nation. Unprovoked, the "noble sport of war" becomes the murder of the innocent.

—*October 2002*

allowing multinational companies to make their most concerted effort in twenty years to roll back clean-air measures, exploit public lands, and stuff the pockets of their executives and shareholders with undeserved subsidies. Against such crass exploitation, unequaled since the Teapot Dome scandal, it is every patriot's duty to join the loyal opposition. Even in war, politics is about who gets what and who doesn't. If the mercenaries and the politicians-for-rent in Washington try to exploit the emergency and America's good faith to grab what they wouldn't get through open debate in peacetime, the disloyalty will be not in our dissent but in our sub-servience. The greatest sedition is silence. Yes, there's a fight going on against terrorists around the globe, but just as certainly there's a fight going on here at home, to decide the kind of country this will be even as we fight the war on terrorism.

What should our strategy be? Here are a couple of suggestions, beginning with how we elect our officials. As Congress debates new security measures, military spending, energy policies, eco-nomic stimulus packages, and various bailout requests, wouldn't it be better if we knew that elected officials had to answer to the people who vote instead of the wealthy individual and corporate donors whose profit or failure may depend on how those new ini-tiatives are carried out?

That's not a utopian notion. Thanks to the efforts of many hardworking pro-democracy activists who have been organizing at the grassroots for the past ten years, we already have four states—Maine, Arizona, Vermont, and Massachusetts—where representatives from governor on down have the option of reject-ing all private campaign contributions and qualifying for full pub-lic financing of their campaigns. About a third of Maine's legislature and a quarter of Arizona's got elected last year running clean. (Under their states' pioneering clean elections systems, they collected a set number of $5 contributions and then pledged to raise no other money and to abide by strict spending limits.)

These unsung heroes of democracy, the first class of elected of-ficials to owe their election solely to their voters and not to any deep-pocketed backers, report a greater sense of independence from special interests and more freedom to speak their minds. "The business lobbyists left me alone," says State Representative Glenn Cummings, a freshman from Maine who was the first can-didate in the country to qualify for clean elections funding. "I think they assumed I was unapproachable. It sure made it easier to get through the hallways on the way to a vote!" His colleague in the statehouse, Senator Ed Youngblood, recalls that running clean changed the whole process of campaigning. "When people would say that it didn't matter how they voted, because legislators would just vote the way the money wants," he tells us, "it was great to be able to say, 'I don't have to vote the way some lobbyist wants just to ensure that I'll get funded by him in two years for reelection.' "

It's too soon to say that money no longer talks in either state capitol, but it clearly doesn't swagger as much. In Maine, the legislature passed a bill creating a Health Security Board tasked with devising a detailed plan to implement a single-payer health care system for the state. The bill wasn't everything its sponsor, Representative Paul Volenik, wanted, but he saw real progress toward a universal health care system in its passage. Two years ago, he noted, only 55 members of the House of Representatives (out of 151) voted for the bill. This time 87 did, including almost all the Democrats and a few Republicans. The bill moved dramatically further, and a portion of that is because of the clean elections system they have there, Volenik said.

The problem is larger than that of money in politics, of course. Democracy needs a broader housecleaning. Consider what a different country we would be if we had a Citizens Channel with a mandate to cover real social problems, not to detail shark attacks or Gary Condit's love life while covering up Rupert Murdoch's manipulations of the FCC and CBS's ploy to filch tax breaks for its post-terrorist losses. Such a channel could have spurred serious attention to the weakness of airport security, for starters, pointing out long ago how the airline industry, through its contributions, had wrung from government the right to contract that security to the lowest bidder. It might have pushed the issue of offshore banking havens to page one, or turned up the astonishing deceit of the

North American Free Trade Agreement provision that enables secret tribunals to protect the interests of investors while subverting
the well-being of workers and the health of communities. Such a
channel—committed to news for the sake of democracy—might
also have told how corporations and their alumni in the Bush
administration have thwarted the development of clean, home-
grown energy that would slow global warming and the degradation of our soil, air, and water while reducing our dependence on
oligarchs, dictators, and theocrats abroad.

Even now the media elite, with occasional exceptions, remain
indifferent to the hypocrisy of Washington's mercenary class as it
goes about the dirty work of its paymasters. What a contrast to
those men and women who during the weeks of loss and mourn-
ing after September 11 reminded us that the kingdom of the
human heart is large, containing great courage. Much has been
made of the comparison to December 7, 1941. I find it apt. In response to the sneak attack on Pearl Harbor, Americans waged and
won a great war, then came home to make this country more
prosperous and just. It is not beyond this generation to live up to
that example. To do so, we must define ourselves not by the lives
we led until September 11 but by the lives we will lead from now
on. If we seize the opportunity to build a more open society, we
too will ultimately prevail in the challenges ahead, at home and
abroad. But we cannot win this new struggle by military might
alone. We will prevail abroad only if we lead by example, as a
democracy committed to the rule of law and the spirit of fairness,
whose corporate and political elites recognize that it isn't only
firefighters, police, and families grieving their missing kin who are
called upon to sacrifice.

—*November 2001*

CROSSING THE EUPHRATES

A headline I saw on the Web, "Marines Cross Euphrates," got me to thinking. Do they know, these young marines, this elite American fighting force? Do they know Alexander the Great crossed the Euphrates, too, on his way to battle and empire, with his engineers, architects, scientists, and scribes and an army forty thousand strong, their thirteen-foot spears gleaming in the sun? The mighty Darius also crossed the Euphrates and on these plains met Alexander in battle. Xenophon, Xerxes, and Sennacherib crossed it, too. The Sumerians crossed this river, as did the Akkadians, Hittites, and Amorites—the Semites as well.

The Euphrates is the largest and longest river of western Asia, and the place where it meets its sister the Tigris became the fertile womb of Mesopotamia, birthplace of civilization. A thousand gods sprang forth here—and cities such as Persepolis, Seleucia, Ninevah, and Babylon. Somewhere between these rivers lay the Garden written of in Genesis. Adam and Eve, exiled, crossed the Euphrates fleeing Eden. Writing first appeared here. Myths and legends took hold: Gilgamesh, the Flood, the prophet Jonah, the Tower of Babel. Sargon, beloved of Ishtar, won thirty-four battles here, ruled twice as many cities, and vanquished his foes. Inanna, goddess of love and war, slaked her thirst and passion here. Hammurabi proclaimed his code. . . .

On the surviving stones is all that remains of conquests, rebellions, and battles, the violent death of rulers, prisoners of war disposed of by execution. For five thousand years the story repeats itself: the victory of one, the defeat of the other. Tribes and gods turn on each other. Omens fill the literature: "A powerful man will ascend the throne in a foreign city," it is written. "They will lock the city gates and there will be calamity in the city." Even Genghis Khan met his match trying to get here.

The last word here has always been written in the sand. Cities and states lie buried beneath it. The great figures who once held sway here—Ashurnasirpal II, Tigllath-pileser III, Shamshi-Adad V, King Ninus and Queen Semiramis, King Shar-kali-sharri, Suleyman the Magnificent, the Ottomans, the British—have all been carried away with the drifting dust.

Five thousand years from now, who will be crossing the Euphrates? What will remain from our time? And what will be remembered?

—*March 2003*

Part Two

THE SOUL OF DEMOCRACY

THE DECLARATION IN OUR TIMES

What can I say about the Declaration of Independence that hasn't already been said? How does a mere journalist do justice to the power and poetry of the words in that document? Sometimes I think we should just kneel in front of it.

I know: many people have a problem with the Declaration in its eighteenth-century context. They consider it discriminatory, exclusionary, and offensive to women, blacks, and minorities. Right now there is a ruckus in New Jersey, where the state legislature has before it a bill that would require schoolchildren to begin classes with the Pledge of Allegiance followed by a passage of the Declaration: "We hold these truths to be self-evident, that all men are created equal. . . ." One New Jersey Democrat says that speaking those words would be repugnant to little girls, and a state senator says black children should not have to repeat the words of a wealthy slave-owning southerner. I understand those feelings; they come from deep wounds. I might have a hard time repeating them, too, if my ancestors had been torn from their family, sold on the block, scarred by the lash, and worked like animals. Surely it galls a person to have your neighbor revere as sacred a document whose author denied your own humanity while becoming a god-like hero in the national pantheon.

But I'd welcome the chance, were I a teacher in New Jersey, to hold up the Declaration to my students and say to them, "Listen, children, now we're going to read *between* the lines." Between the lines is a story that takes us deeper into the human condition and the American experience than any civics book. Think very hard about this. The hands that wrote these words also stroked the breasts and caressed the thighs of a slave woman named Sally Hemings. The same voice that read those words aloud by candle-light to other patriots whispered in the slave woman's ear other words far too intimate for parchment. This slave woman—who was the half sister of his late wife—bore him six children. How do we know? DNA tells us. Exhaustive historical research and foren-sic investigation support it, and not even the Thomas Jefferson Memorial Foundation denies it. It's true: the man who wrote these noble words had a long-term sexual relationship with his slave, and the children she bore by him—his children—were slaves themselves. One guest at Monticello who looked up at dinner one evening was startled to see a young servant who was the spitting image of the master at the table.

Jefferson never acknowledged those children as his own, and as he grew older he relied more and more on slavery to keep him afloat financially. When he died his slaves were sold to satisfy his creditors—all except Sally. She, through an obscure passage in Jef-ferson's will, was the only slave at Monticello to secure the free-dom of her children. Two of those children settled in Ohio, where their own descendants increased during the years, some living as blacks and some as whites. Two centuries later race still divides them. Some consider themselves black, though they look white, and some consider themselves white, although they have known black ancestors. The family of one white descendant turned on her when she decided to seek out her relatives among the black Hemingses. And bitter feelings have risen of late because those black Hemingses want membership in the Jefferson Family Association and the right to be buried in the Jefferson family cemetery.

So I would tell these New Jersey children that Jefferson got it right when he wrote these noble words about life, liberty, and the pursuit of happiness. He had to know the flesh-and-blood woman in his arms was his equal in her desire for life, her longing for liberty, her passion for happiness. My friend Mortimer Adler once said of the Declaration that whatever things are really good for any human beings are really good for all other human beings. The happy or good life is essentially the same for all: a satisfaction of the same needs inherent in human nature. Yet all Sally Hemings got from her long sufferance—perhaps it was all she sought from what may have grown into a secret and unacknowledged love—was that he let her children go. This he did at death for them, but not for his other slaves. He needed the money. He got it right, you see, but he lived it wrong. He got it right for the same reason he lived it wrong: he was human. So addicted to intellect that it overruled his heart, so enthralled to place and privilege that he could send the noblest sentiments winging around the world but not allow them to lodge in his own house, so much a creature of his times was he that even when he knew the truth, he lived the lie. Thomas Jefferson embodies the oldest and longest war of all, the war of the self. It is what Saul of Tarsus, who became the Apostle Paul, understood when he wrote: "I do not do what I want to—and what I detest, I do." It is what Emily Dickinson understood when she wrote:

> I felt a cleaving in my mind,
> As if my brain had split—
> I tried to match it seam by seam—
> But could not make it fit.

What I would want these children in New Jersey to know is this: the man who wrote the words of the Declaration understood a great truth. No man is fit to be a master. Prince, pope, politician, plantation overseer: whoever puts on the brief cloak of power is reluctant to take it off again. Left to their own devices, monarchs, masters, and ministers (of state or church) will define the meaning of things by edict and resolve conflicts by fiat, concealing their own self-interest in platitudes of piety.

Jefferson's Declaration proclaimed an end to arbitrary rule, and the Revolution produced a republic where the consent of the governed meant that from now on the powers that be, the elites, would have to live up to their words or eat them. Now it would be up to the people themselves to define what these words would mean in the real world of politics. Since this document replaced biblical law with natural law, there would be no fixed, dogmatic criteria to which the people would appeal for guidance and no authority apart from themselves upon whom they could rely. We were on our own. Even Sally Hemings' descendants would one day have their say.

So I would tell these students in New Jersey that we don't have to whitewash our history. Last year, around the Fourth of July, Hollywood released a Mel Gibson blockbuster, *The Patriot*. The producers felt compelled to rewrite the story in order to have the Americans voting to free the slaves who fought for the colonies, when in fact exactly the opposite happened. It was the British who offered the slaves their freedom and the Americans who enforced slavery's laws without exception. The movie gave historians heartburn; uncritical patriots loved it, for the truth is too much for them.

Yes, the Declaration is a truly grand and farsighted document, inspiring and prophetic. Once let loose those ideas could not be caged again. In time slaves would invoke these very words to assert their right to freedom. Even so, it still took a bloody civil war to free them and another hundred years after that for their descendants to achieve the vote. Oppression is stubborn, ignorance resilient. Jefferson knew this and didn't believe that the promise of the Declaration could be realized in one generation.

Hoping they will carry on the struggle, I would tell this class in New Jersey a story. Recently, approaching the age of ninety, Doris Haddock set out to walk across America to protest the subversion of democracy by money in politics. Ten miles every day, sometimes with blistered feet and bruised muscles, she walked. She had her doubts about the journey. "Chasing my hat again through cacti, the idea of walking across the United States at my age seemed a less than perfect idea. I was being foolish: the country is too big for an old New Hampshire woman with arthritis and emphysema and parched lips and a splintered hat." But since her activist days in the 1960s she had watched American politics change. Back then, she says, "we were able to appeal to the sense of faith of U.S. Senators and Representatives. They listened to our appeal and made a decision they thought best. They did not have to consult with their campaign contributors nor did they care that we had not given money to them." It was not a perfect world, she said, "but the backroom scandals we heard about then, where cash was traded for votes, are now the front room norm. There is no room for regular citizens and there is no shame." She and some friends had spent a lot of time studying the matter; what they learned about how democracy is being purchased from under us put her on the road.

At first the national media paid little attention, dismissing her as an eccentric old woman and her journey as a stunt. But no sooner had she started collecting petition signatures in Santa Monica, before heading west toward the Mojave Desert, than ordinary people perked up and paid attention, moved by what this cheerful, straight-talking Yankee was saying:

If money is speech, then those with more money have more speech, and that idea is antithetical to a democracy that cherishes political fairness. It makes us no longer equal citizens. A flood of special interest money has carried away our representatives, and all that is left of them—at least for those of us who do not write $100,000 checks—are the shadows of their cardboard cutouts. It is said that democracy is not something we have, but something we do. But right now, we cannot do it because we cannot speak. We are shouted down by the bullhorns of big money. It is money with no manners for democracy, and it must be escorted from the room. The hundreds of thousands of our dead, buried in rows upon rows in our national cemeteries, sacrificed their lives for the democracy of a free people, not for what we have today. It is up to each of us to see that these boys and girls did not die in vain. That's just how serious this message is.

On and on she walked: through the blowing sands of Arizona, past the reddish hills of New Mexico, toward the vast plains of West Texas. Like tom-toms local radio stations and newspapers signaled her advance. Cars began honking, thumbs went up. Children from their playground monkey bars chanted, "Gran-ny. Gran-ny." Fraternity boys knelt around her on a street corner in Tucson and made her a sweetheart of Sigma Chi. Swarthy tattooed bikers on their Harley-Davidsons offered her protection on the highways. Strangers took her in, providing food and encouragement. "I had found so many new friends along the road," she said, "and they had entrusted me with so much of their hearts, that I was not feeling the least bit alone anymore." She was even greeted in Parker, Arizona, by the Marine Corps Marching Band.

People lined up to listen, ask questions, and tell their own stories of political abandonment. They told of hitting the wall that connects HMOs and drug companies, "all in cahoots with crooked politicians," of writing urgent petitions only to receive form letters in return, of corporations using their overpowering capital and political influence to annihilate small business, turning towns into colonies.

The *New York Times* showed up, and soon the media flocked alongside. Strangers flew from distant parts to walk with her. In Little Rock she stopped at Central High School, where one of the first great battles over integration occurred, and spoke at the First Missionary Baptist Church, where Martin Luther King Jr. once preached; at first the congregation eyed her suspiciously, but they ended up on their feet, cheering. In Memphis she traced King's last march and made a speech that had the audience weeping and clapping. In Louisville she entered the lions' den—the office of Senator Mitch McConnell, the ardent apologist for legalized bribery. In Cumberland, Maryland, near the log cabin that was Washington's headquarters during the Whiskey Rebellion, she celebrated her ninetieth birthday with a large crowd escorting her through town, carrying flags and singing, "This land is your land."

In Washington, D.C., after a Scottish bagpiper had led her past the Lincoln and Washington Memorials, down K Street's lobbyist row to the Capitol Building, Granny D. made one more speech.

> Along my three thousand miles through the heart of America, did I meet anyone who thought that their voice as an equal citizen now counts for much in the corrupt halls of Washington? No, I did not. Did I meet anyone who felt anger or pain over this? I did indeed, and I watched them shake with rage sometimes when they spoke, and I saw tears well up in their eyes. The people I met along my way have given me messages to deliver here. The messages are many, written with old and young hands of every color, and yet the messages are the same. They are this: "Shame on you, Senators and Congressmen, who have turned the headquarters of a great and self-serving people into a bawdyhouse." The time for this shame is ending.

Then Granny D. got herself arrested: for reading the Declaration of Independence in a calm voice in the Rotunda of the Capitol. She wanted to make the point, she said, "that we must declare our independence from campaign corruption."

Did America hear? Judging by the returns of the 2000 election, we might say no. It was by far the most expensive election in our history, a quantum leap of nearly 50 percent from the scandalously costly election of 1996. You might think Doris Haddock walked across America for nothing. Not so. John McCain and Bill Bradley read her speeches and watched how she succeeded in making campaign reform a patriotic issue with many Americans. When Albert Gore finally signed on to campaign finance reform, his speech cited McCain, Bradley—and Doris Haddock. No one did more to give energy to the issue, to bring together right and left, white and black, old and young, in the next great round of the American Revolution. "It is clear to me," Doris Haddock writes in her book, "that people feel oppressed by Big Money politicians and take glee in any chance for a small rebellion. Now the fight between the human scale and giant scale—between the master and the governed—left unresolved by the Progressive Era, is returning for some kind of epic confrontation." Sometimes, says Doris Haddock, "all you can do is put your body in front of a problem and stand there as a witness to it."

Thomas Jefferson knew that it would be necessary for each generation not only to cherish and preserve the Declaration's heritage of freedom but to enlarge and extend its reach, until the children of slaves—his own children—became the sons and daughters of liberty. The work goes on. Now it's our turn.

—2000

MANY FAITHS, ONE NATION

As we are often reminded, for most of our history this country's religious discourse was dominated by white male Protestants of a culturally conservative European heritage—people like me. Dissenting visions of America, alternative visions of faith, of race, of women, rarely reached the mainstream. The cartoonist Jeff McNally summed it up with two weirdos talking in a California diner. One weirdo says to the other, "Have you ever delved into the mysteries of Eastern religion?" And the second weirdo answers: "Yes, I was once a Methodist in Philadelphia." Once upon a time that was about the extent of our exposure to the varieties of religious experience, but it's different now.*

When I moved to New York in 1968 I was impressed to see people on the subway reading the Hebrew Bible, to see people reading the Bible in Spanish. I'd never seen that in Marshall, Texas. When I ride the subway today I'm just as likely to see someone reading the Koran as the Bible. Although the figures are disputed, there are more Muslims in America than Episcopalians or Presby-

---

* For some of these insights I am especially indebted to Diane Eck, whose Pluralism Project at Harvard University has documented the contours of the new religious landscape in America and earned the gratitude of all of us who are trying to come to terms with an unprecedented phenomenon.

terians, and within a few years there may be more Muslims than Jews. One day I read that Muslims are the fastest-growing religion in America, then that Pentecostals are, then that the fastest-growing Christian denomination is the Church of Jesus Christ of Latter Day Saints (the Mormons), whose membership has been doubling every fifteen years since World War II.

When I was growing up, nurture and culture told me I belonged to the one true religion. Then I discovered that every religion conveys possible ways of expressing human experience and self-understanding. Because each religion can appear utterly incomprehensible to the others, however, we are facing what Gerald Bruns describes as a "contest of narratives," with more meanings "than we know what to do with."

Our nation is being re-created right before our eyes. Travel the country, writes Diane Eck, and you see an America dotted with mosques, in places such as Toledo, Phoenix, and Atlanta. You come upon huge Hindu temples in Pittsburgh, Albany, and California's Silicon Valley. There are Sikh communities in Stockton, California, and Queens, New York, and Buddhist retreat centers in the mountains of Vermont and West Virginia. A Buddhist American died on the *Challenger*. A Muslim American is mayor of a town in my native state of Texas. Hindu Americans are now managers at Boston Edison and Procter & Gamble.

The world's religious landscape is changing, too. As Gustav Niebuhr has reported in the *New York Times,* Christianity is no longer "a predominantly Western religion." In what is a monumental shift in the ecclesiastical center of gravity, the majority of Christians now live outside Europe and North America. For example, the *World Christian Encyclopedia* documents the fascinating migration of the Moravians, whose roots run to Central Europe and to American communities that date to the eighteenth century. Of the seven hundred thousand Moravians worldwide, half are in East Africa: in Tanzania, the annual membership increase is more than the total Moravian membership of fifty thousand in the United States. Furthermore, Niebuhr wrote, there are more missionaries at work today than ever before in history, of whom at least one hundred thousand are being sent out by Protestant churches in non-Western countries. Korea alone has some eight thousand Protestant missionaries serving outside the country!

I would like to be around to cover the consequences of this mobility as the changes multiply. We do not know how the world's religions will coexist as they take root in America. In my optimistic moments I imagine all of us mindful of that verse in the Koran that says: "If we had wished, we could have made you one people, but as it is, we have made you many. Therefore, vie among yourselves in good works." But optimism may be wishful thinking. Although we Americans pride ourselves on not only tolerating but also celebrating diversity, as a Protestant culture we preached tolerance more than we practiced it. So we have to ask: can we avoid the intolerance, the chauvinism, the fanaticism, the bitter fruits that occur when different religions rub up against each other?

It's no rhetorical question. The scholar of religion, Elaine Pagels, told me in an interview that "there's practically no religion I know of that sees other people in a way that affirms the others' choice." This is the case even within denominations that share common roots. I grew up in that big tent of tradition called Baptists. At last count, there were more than two dozen varieties of Baptists in America. They include Bill Clinton and Pat Robertson. Jesse Jackson is a Baptist; so is Jesse Helms. Al Gore is a Baptist; so is Trent Lott. Newt Gingrich is a Baptist; so is Richard Gephardt. No wonder Baptists have been compared to jalapeño peppers: one or two make for a tasty dish, but a whole bunch of them together in one place brings tears to your eyes. We Baptists differ profoundly in how we read the Bible, how we read history, how we read the separation of church and state, and how we read election results.

In the real world of democracy, how do we cope with a thousand local gods? How do I hold my truth to be *the* truth when everyone else sees truth differently? I put this question to the renowned scholar of comparative religion Huston Smith, who has spent the whole of his adult life trying to penetrate the essence of the world's great religions. He wrote, "Religions are like rivers, dynamic and changing, bearing the heritage of the past to water the fields of the present. These rivers are converging and we need to build bridges." When I asked him how we are to do this, he replied: "We listen. We listen as alertly to the other person's description of reality as we hope they listen to us."

Listening can be scary. Some people fear that hearing what others have to say about faith will lead to the loss of their own distinctive tradition: that they may have to shed the uniqueness of their own beliefs to embrace a flimsy ecumenism in which all religions are reduced to saying the same thing. They even imagine they will be dragged into accepting some vapid consensus of "one faith for one world."

It doesn't have to be that way; that certainly wasn't the experience in our PBS series on Genesis. This was a simple series by television's standard—seven people facing each other in a circle of conversation—but nothing I had produced for television until then had created more media response prior to broadcast than did those ten discussions. At its best, conversation is, as Thomas Moore has written, "the interpretation of worlds," so my colleagues and I wanted to be sure our participants in the series didn't come from the same neighborhood. Talking with people who agree with you is like jogging in a cul-de-sac. When I was growing up in East Texas, Baptists talked about the Bible with Baptists,

Presbyterians with Presbyterians, Episcopalians with Episcopalians, Methodists with Methodists, and Jews with Jews. But we
never talked about the Bible across our faiths, much less across our
races. So for the series we sought out people from varied backgrounds, faiths, professional fields, ages, and genders. We wanted to
see if they could be candid about their different beliefs without
politicizing religion or polarizing the community. We hoped to
show that you can disagree passionately about things that matter
without surrendering your own principled beliefs or without
going for your neighbor's throat; that Americans can engage with
others in serious conversation about the most deeply felt subjects—our religious beliefs, the nature of faith, our relationship
with each other—and truly challenge each other, teach each
other, and learn from each other. It worked; all over the country
people organized into groups so they could watch the programs
together and then talk about them afterward. One organization
alone signed up a million people just for this purpose.

This, despite the fact that beforehand we were repeatedly
warned that Americans didn't want to hear God-talk on television. Perhaps this explains why, although nine out of ten Americans tell George Gallup they've never doubted the existence of
God, it's hard to hear God mentioned in mainstream media except
by somebody who's trying to put something over on you. William
F. Buckley has said that if you mention God once at a dinner in
New York, you'll be greeted with silence, but if you mention God
a second time, you'll never be invited back. We wanted to test that
idea, to see if people would come back week after week to hear
other people talking publicly about God from different perspec-
tives.

We couldn't have had better material. Genesis offers the power
of great storytelling—of characters as complex as any you'll ever
meet in literature. Three major faiths trace their origins to these

stories. They are the quintessential Jewish story. We Christians have adopted them to our canon. Muslims trace their beginnings back to the departure from Abraham's camp of Hagar and the child born of their union, Ishmael. For three faiths Genesis is a documentary of the founding generation, and yet these very old stories speak across the generations with characters who are starkly human. They rage at one another and at God. They're schemers and dreamers and parents who play favorites and children who run away from home. Here are tales of willful sons and estranged siblings and troubled marriages, with lots of envy, lust, infertility, and deception—all of the elements we would describe today as dysfunctional behavior. Here are these people like us, trying to figure out how to live with each other and answer to an eccentric and erratic divinity.

One of my favorite stories is one of the most bizarre, and therefore most human: the story of Noah. When I was a kid in Sunday school at the Central Baptist Church in Marshall, we didn't have baseball cards; we had Bible cards depicting scenes from the scriptures. The Bible card with Noah I remember especially: Mr. and Mrs. Noah sitting on the prow of the ark, gazing out toward the horizon at the beautiful rainbow arching across the sky, all the animals gathered around with little smiley faces. It was the perfect children's story, a real American tale with a setting and ending suitable for Walt Disney.

But this is no children's story. It raises hard questions about adult behavior. If Noah knew what was coming, why didn't he alert his neighbors—or at least his in-laws? The fundamentalists will tell you it was because Noah was being obedient to God. He was just doing what he was told. But we have to ask: does obedience carry with it the negation of mercy? Was there no pity in his heart for those in the path of the Flood? Was he so intent upon establishing the first chapter of the Society for the Prevention of

Cruelty to Animals that he didn't have any concern for his fellow human beings?

Karen Armstrong reminded our group that the original title of the novel on which the film *Schindler's List* is based was *Schindler's Ark*. The author, Thomas Keneally, thought the image of the ark was appropriate for Oskar Schindler's factory, where he saved hundreds of intended victims of the Nazi Holocaust. Schindler was no righteous man in the conventional sense of the word; he was a playboy and philanderer, the kind of fellow God would probably have drowned back in Noah's day. And yet Oskar Schindler risked his life to rescue the doomed and the damned. Most of his contemporaries behaved like Noah. They blocked out all knowledge of the carnage, obeying their superiors in order to save themselves, trying to ride out the storm in safety. I was confronted during that discussion by a very hard question: if I had been raised not in Marshall, Texas, during the early thirties but in Munich, Germany, would I, as a Christian, have tried to save anyone?

These stories present us with tough questions. How do we interpret Noah's conduct after the Flood? He was clearly traumatized when he got off the boat. The first thing he did was to build an altar. All the preachers I heard as a kid said this confirmed his righteousness, proving he deserved to be saved. But just a few verses later Noah gets drunk, curses his children, and abuses his grandson. No sooner does God save the man, giving humanity a second chance, than the rainbow fades into alcoholism and child abuse. Tough questions indeed. In many ways, I've come to think of Noah as the quintessential twentieth-century figure. In the Jewish mystical teachings, the Kabbalah, the world never really escaped the devastation of the Flood. It represents, metaphorically, the dilemmas of contemporary society. Its waters rage all around us—and within us.

And what about God in this story? I was taught that God saved Noah as an act of compassion. But Jack Miles paints a different picture. Miles won the Pulitzer Prize for his book *God: A Biography,* and he tells us this is not the story of a good God saving a good man from a natural disaster. This is the story of a good God saving a good man from a bad God. And the horror of the story is that the good God and the bad God are one and the same.

In the first chapter of Genesis, not once but seven times God says of creation, "It's good," yet just six chapters and ten generations later, God is so appalled by the violence and the corruption of humanity that God drowns everyone except for Noah and his family and the animals they could get on the ark. Were there no other children in the neighborhood? What does it say that we have come to revere a story that has no place for the unelected? The God of Genesis, says Jack Miles, is a God of radical unpredictability, combining immense physical power with terrifying moral ambivalence. We get in the silences of this text the question that haunts our own genocidal times. Why must the innocent suffer, and what does this mean for faith? One of our participants in the series told of the Jews condemned to die in the concentration camp at Auschwitz. Day after day they were marched into the gas chambers. But one day the survivors decided they'd had enough. They decided that God must be tried for having let all this horror happen. They convened a tribunal. They heard all the evidence. They passed their judgment. They pronounced God guilty and sentenced God to die. No sooner was the judgment rendered than one old rabbi got up and said, "All right, the trial is over. It's time for the evening prayer." At the heart of deep faith is an old contradiction: "I believe. Help Thou my unbelief."

One of our most fascinating discussions centered on the story of Cain and Abel. Adam and Eve are the first parents to discover what it means to raise Cain. They have a second son named Abel. Both boys want to please God, so both bring God offerings. Cain is a farmer and offers the first fruits of the soil. Abel is a shepherd and offers the first lamb from the flock: two very generous gifts. God, playing favorites, chooses Abel's offering over Cain's, and the elevation of the younger leads to the humiliation of the elder. Cain is so jealous he strikes out at his brother and kills him.

Here is the first paradox we confronted in our discussion: Abel is innocent, and yet Abel dies. If you saw the broadcast, you know that at this particular point, the novelist Mary Gordon, a struggling Catholic, says, "This is the hopeless moment: the realization that goodness and purity do not protect you. It did not protect the Jews. It did not protect the Africans sold into slavery. It did not protect the Native Americans. Goodness and purity of heart," she said, "are irrelevant to your fate and punishment. In the end, Abel is dead. And dead is dead, and God did nothing about it." This is the narrative moment, says Mary Gordon, "when doubt becomes absolutely comprehensible and almost inevitable." But she goes on to express poignantly what it means to be a survivor. For Mary Gordon, the challenge for a moral person is always to be a witness to Abel. To be an ethical human being, she believes, is to say, "I'm in the place of that person unjustly cut down. I am a witness to that."

Here's the second paradox. The first murder arose out of a religious act. Both brothers are rivals for God's favor. Their rivalry leads to violence and ends in death. Once this pattern is established, it's played out in the story of Isaac and Ishmael, Jacob and Esau, Joseph and his brothers, and down through the centuries in generation after generation of conflict between Muslims and Jews, Jews and Christians, Christians and Muslims, so that the red trail of religiously spilled blood runs directly from east of Eden to

Beirut to Bosnia to Belfast to every place in the world where the compassion of brothers and believers, of sisters and seekers, turns to competition and violence. The author of *In Praise of Religious Diversity,* James Wiggins, says that virtually every armed conflict occurring on the planet today is explicitly driven by religious motives or by memory traces of persisting religious conflict. We get fundamentalists in Algeria who want to make their country an Islamic theocracy shooting teenage girls in the face for not wearing a veil, and cutting professors' throats for teaching male and female students in the same classroom. We get Muslim suicide bombers killing busloads of Jews, and a fanatical Jewish doctor with a machine gun mowing down thirty praying Muslims in a mosque. We get the young Orthodox Jew who assassinated Yitzhak Rabin declaring on television, "Everything I did, I did for the glory of God." Hindus and Muslims slaughter one another in India. In America, Muslims bomb New York's World Trade Center in order to smite the Great Satan; Timothy McVeigh blows up the federal building in Oklahoma City, killing 168 people, in part as revenge against the government for killing David Koresh and his followers. Groups calling themselves the Christian Identity Movement and the Christian Patriot League collect arsenals, and at a political convention in Dallas not long ago, at a so-called Christian booth in the exhibit hall, you could buy an apron with two pockets: one for the Bible and one for a gun. Religion has a healing side, we know this, but religion also has a killing side. In William Penn's words, "To be furious in religion is to be furiously irreligious."

Who among us might not cast the first stone? In our television discussions of Cain and Abel, Mary Gordon admitted, "It's quite remarkable I'm not behind bars. I find trying not to be a murderer completely grueling." We laughed, but she caused us to realize how these stories reveal the tendencies in each of us to obey contradictory impulses—a condition that constantly challenges democracy.

On a recent visit with our grandchildren in Minneapolis, I arose early one morning and was drinking my coffee in the kitchen, reading the newspaper, when Thomas, who was then two, came down the stairs. Thomas likes his cereal straight, so I poured his Cheerios out on the high chair tray. We talked intermittently while I read and he amused himself with his cereal and imagination. About half an hour later Henry, who was four, came down: the gentle blue-eyed child with the sweet and sensitive face. When he came into the room and saw his younger brother, he didn't say, "Hi, Thomas." He said, "Thomas, I'm going to kill you!" Now, this is a household where watching television is at a minimum. He didn't hear this kind of talk from his parents or his grandparents. Where did the notion come from? What is this primal impulse to wither a brother that can surface so quickly?

These stories don't always have happy endings or provide easy answers. They force us to confront our own quandaries without pat solutions. In my childhood the characters in the Bible were ten feet tall. In seminary I studied these stories to learn the answers to questions that I would be asked later by classrooms or congregations. But life has a way of questioning your answers; bumpersticker theology and sound-bite philosophy ceased to tell me what I need to know, and I find myself reflected in these people of Genesis. They don't always do the right thing. They don't always even know what the right thing is. They live with ambiguity. Very often they don't know what to make of God, and quite often God doesn't know what to make of them, either.

Often in our series we disagreed, and sometimes the more we talked, the more we disagreed. We were critical and skeptical. No one was dishonest enough to politely let pass a point that called for a challenge. Talking about the issues exposed our differences, but each of us connected to people who had been strangers when we met. Sometimes we discovered that despite our differences we shared some fundamental values with people who seemed most unlike us. We were constantly reminded that differences between faiths are real and shouldn't be papered over for protocol's sake, but we discovered that minds and hearts can be profoundly touched with understanding when you listen to the loves of others.

Which brings me to my personal experience. I am a journalist, but I am also a pilgrim. I believe that within the religious quest—in the deeper realm of spirituality that may well be the primal origin of all religion—lies what Gregg Easterbrook calls "an essential aspect of the human prospect." Here is where we wrestle with questions of life and purpose, of meaning and loss, of yearning and hope. I am grateful to have first been exposed to those questions in my own Christian tradition. T.S. Eliot believed that "no man has ever climbed to the higher stages of the spiritual life who has not been a believer in a particular religion, or at least a particular philosophy." As we dig deeper into our own religion, if we are lucky we break through to someone else digging deeper toward us from the core of their tradition, and on some transcendent level we converge, like the images inside a kaleidoscope, discovering new patterns of faith that illuminate our own journey. I respect the Christian story—my own story—even more for having come to see that all the great religions grapple with things that matter, although each may come out at a different place; that each arises from within and expresses a lived human experience; and that each and every one of them offers a unique insight into human nature.

Buddhists have taught me about the delight of contemplation and "the infinite within." From Muslims I have learned about the nature of surrender, from Jews about the power of the prophetic conscience, from Hindus about "realms of gold hidden in the depth of our hearts," from Confucianists about the empathy necessary to sustain the fragile web of civilization. Nothing I take from them has come at the expense of the Christian story. While I reject the notion that faith is acquired in the same way one chooses a meal in a cafeteria, I confess there is something liberating about no longer being quite so deaf to what others have to report from their experience. They have led me away from condescending toleration of other faiths to an anticipation and affirmation of positive engagement with them. They have led me to the understanding so beautifully expressed by Kathleen Norris in one of her poems when she says, "We are all God's chosen now," and in the next breath prays, "God help us because we are."

The call, you see, is not to pride. The call is to humility. In the words of the Jewish theologian Abraham Joshua Heschel, "No religion is an island. We are all involved with one another. Spiritual betrayal on the part of one affects the faith of all."

Since the series I am often asked to identify my favorite verse in the whole of Genesis. It's the third verse of the second chapter: "God gave the seventh day his blessing and he hallowed it, for on it he ceased from all his work that by creating, God had made." I take this to mean creation is not finished. Life is dynamic, like democracy, continuously in renewal. Genesis is about the beginning. What happens to creation is up to us.

—1998, 2001

THE SOUL OF DEMOCRACY

There are two things that are important in politics," said the wealthy businessman Mark Hanna. "The first is money and I can't remember what the second one is." He didn't need to remember; Hanna was the first modern political fund-raiser, and money was all that mattered to him. He tapped the banks, the insurance companies, the railroads, and the other great industrial trusts of the late 1800s for contributions of some $6–7 million to the campaign of presidential candidate William McKinley: big bucks back then. His Democratic-Populist opponent, William Jennings Bryan, who was perceived as a real challenge to those large economic interests due to his Populist roots, raised one-tenth as much. McKinley won. Money in politics is an old story.

What's new is that it is now the only story. The lid is off: the more money you have, the better your chance of election, so one side escalates and the other follows suit. Today this arms race is undermining the second thing that is important in politics, the thing Mark Hanna said he couldn't remember: democracy. Money has robbed the middle class and the working poor of representation—and as they become weaker politically, they are even more insecure in their jobs, their savings, and their future.

One of the commercial networks commissioned a poll in

which voters were asked, "Do you think our elected representatives are dedicated public servants or lying windbags?" Forty-four percent said that the officials were a bunch of lying windbags. Just 36 percent said they thought elected officials were dedicated public servants. This was true regardless of their party; Republicans, Democrats, and independents alike see a bunch of lying windbags in Washington, D.C. And when asked who really controls Washington, respondents overwhelmingly answered, "Special interests." Nearly everyone surveyed thinks contributions affect the voting behavior of members of Congress. In another poll only 14 percent of the people gave members of Congress a high rating for honesty and ethical standards. This is what politics has become in the popular perception: a bunch of self-interested, lying windbags on the take from moneyed special interests.

There is an important warning here. Millions of Americans are alienated, apathetic, and disillusioned about politics. Fewer than half of us bother to vote at all in our presidential elections—compared to 80 percent a century ago—and only about one-third vote in our congressional elections. People will tell you they feel betrayed, sold out by a political class of professional electioneers, big donors, lobbyists, and the media. What happens when so many people drop out of a system they no longer respect and which they think no longer represents them? Democracy loses its legitimacy.

THE GREAT WONDER of American democracy has been its openness to change. "Two Cheers for Democracy," wrote E.M. Forster, "one because it admits variety and two because it permits criticism." With one tragic exception—the Civil War—we have been able to resolve our differences through the political process. Women demanded the right to vote and finally got it. Workers demanded the right to organize and finally got it. Blacks demanded political and legal equality and finally got it. It is true that in each of these cases protest began on the streets, outside the electoral system, and many lives were sacrificed in these struggles, but ultimately the political system responded. Democracy won out.

What I find troubling today is democracy's inability to resolve some of the critical issues that face our nation. These questions—all the more critical because of the growing disparities of wealth in this country—are almost entirely off the screen of public debate. Only a rare reporter like Thomas Edsall *(The New Politics of Inequality)* writes about how changes in the political process have strengthened the power of the affluent and eroded the power of the poor, the working class, and the lower-middle class. These are not the subjects wealthy contributors want their politicians to talk about, and journalists who work for mainstream corporate media lack the independence to make such issues the stuff of the news. We get from them, instead, endless soap operas of nonsense, trivia, celebrity, and violence. There is plenty of news for consumers but too little for citizens. Suppose we are struck by a new and potentially paralyzing crisis, of the kind democracies inevitably encounter. What happens if people no longer feel like shareholders in the venture, no longer care about the integrity of the political process, no longer think it's their democracy?

I argue often that the soul of democracy is "government of, by, and for the people." Not all of the people can govern, of course, not even in theory—not in a nation this vast and diverse. Besides, "the people" are not always virtuous, intelligent, or wise; sometimes, as Henry Miller reminds us, "the blind lead the blind. That's democracy." No, government "of, by, and for the people" enshrines two bedrock ideas that animate our political system: representation and political equality. We believe our best chance at governing ourselves lies in obtaining the considered judgments of those we elect to represent us. Having cast our votes, we expect those officials to weigh the competing interests and decide to the best of their ability what is right for the Republic. Second is the notion—as FDR put it in 1936—that "inside the polling booth every American man and woman stands as the equal of every other American man and woman. There they have no superiors. There they have no masters save their own minds and consciences." This ability to arrive at what is good for the nation enables us to describe democracy as "the rule of the ruled." For this Americans of all stripes have sacrificed, strived, suffered, and died, in the belief that all citizens should have an equal political footing on the ground of democracy.

But the arms race of money overwhelms that faith. No one has said it better than Senator Barry Goldwater in 1987:

> The fact that liberty depended on honest elections was of the utmost importance to the patriots who founded our nation and wrote the Constitution. They knew that corruption destroyed the prime requisite of constitutional liberty, an independent legislature free from any influence other than that of the people. Applying these principles to modern times, we can make the following conclusions. To be successful, representative government assumes that elections will be controlled by the citizenry at large, not by those who give the most money. Electors must believe their vote counts. Elected officials must owe their allegiance to the people, not to their own wealth or to the wealth of interest groups who speak only for the selfish fringes of the whole community.

Spoken like a true conservative. But tell that to Roger Tamraz, the oilman who gave large contributions to President Reagan— large enough to earn "Republican Eagle" status—and then made a $300,000 donation to the Democratic party to get a moment at Bill Clinton's ear. He wanted the president to support a pipeline from Russia to the Mediterranean Sea that would have given him control of exports from the Caspian Sea, the richest undeveloped pool of oil left on earth. His largesse got him called before Senate hearings on campaign finance, where his candor made him a star. His money, he said, had produced potential benefits for him far beyond the pipeline project. He hoped it might someday lead to a foreign policy post. After all, he noted, "a lot of our Cabinet ministers and a lot of our ambassadors" have been large donors. The senators tried to play it straight. They fumed. They expressed outrage. At one point Senator Fred Thompson boomed, "Do you think you have a constitutional right to have your business deal considered personally by the president of the United States?" Tamraz shot back, "Senator, I go to the outer limits. Why not? You set the rules and we're following. This is politics as usual." Then came the punch line: in a final effort to shake him, one senator asked Tamraz if he had ever voted or registered to vote. No, he replied, "I think [money] is a bit more than a vote."

A moment of truth in politics. Consider: recently, when Congress finally voted an increase in the minimum wage, the increase was minuscule, but at least it went to the working stiffs on the low rung of the ladder. Nevertheless, Congress and the White House couldn't even do this little bit for ordinary folks without sneaking in a big bonus for the privileged: tax breaks worth $20 billion to an array of wealthy corporations. The sweet deal, like so many others, was hidden down in the fine print amidst the arcane language, where the secret is safe until the damage is done.

Roger Tamraz was right that "money is a bit more than a vote." But while organized economic interests have legitimate claims in the public realm and deserve to be heard, democracy depends upon the balance between organized money and organized people: the two ways to wield influence in our society. Right now the scales are greatly tipped in favor of big money, as the richest interests in America have harnessed their resources for the protection of their privileges. Newt Gingrich changed his tune once he came to power and put the GOP and House of Representatives on the auction block, but once upon a time, when he was younger and out of power, he believed that "Congress is increasingly a system of corruption in which money politics is defeating and driving out citizen politics."

What happens to our venerable experiment in self-rule if it is money that rules our politics, and what can we do about it? Let's not talk for the moment in terms of soft money, hard money, independent expenditures, issue ads, coordinated expenditures, compliance expenditures, express advocacy, in-kind contributions, party committees, multi-candidate committees, nonconnected committees, nonparty committees, political action committees, and so on. I am convinced that this language exists, in the main, to make us glaze over in boredom and incomprehension in the hopes that we will stop poking into the politician's real business.

In entering such a looking-glass world we lose the ability to call the most basic transaction by its right name. If a baseball player stepping up to home plate were to lean over and hand the umpire a wad of bills before the pitch, we would know what that was: a bribe. But when a real estate developer buys his way into the White House with big bucks and gets a favorable government ruling that wouldn't be available to you or me, or when the tobacco industry stuffs $13 million in the pockets of the merry looters in Congress and gets protection in return, we call that a campaign contribution. It is bribery, nonetheless, and it is steadily robbing our political system of legitimacy. Therein lies the tragedy. I want to believe most politicians run for office for honorable reasons. They want to make a difference. They are not as a group any more corrupted than the rest of us, but because politics is now an arms race, they have to raise huge sums of money just to finance their campaigns. Now it is a "wealth primary" that decides who is a viable candidate. Once in office, the victors want to stay there, and now they are introduced to the very different language in Washington that describes much more accurately the real terms of endearment in government today: cash constituents, cashing in, conflicts of interest, corruption, dialing for dollars, fat cats, honest graft, influence peddling, interested money, loopholes, money chase, quid pro quo, regulatory exemptions, subsidies, tax breaks, and vested interests. They have tied their fate to a relative handful of rich contributors and powerful interests that supply the money in exchange for favors. No wonder Ellen Miller, the founding director of the Center for Responsive Politics, jokes that if your daughter wants to become president, you'd better make her next birthday present a fund-raiser.

I CAME TO SEE the crisis of money in politics more acutely a few years ago when Robert and Ford Schumann asked me to take on the presidency of the Schumann Foundation, a progressive foundation based in New Jersey that had been pursuing a variety of public interests, among them education, civil rights, and the environment. It had become apparent to the Schumanns that just about every concern of their grant making, especially the environment, was being frustrated by the influence of private money over public policy. Many grantees were grassroots citizens standing up to polluters in their communities, but even when they could claim the high moral ground they were often trumped by the power of money as they tried to codify their success into state law. Donors with access and more clout than mere voters were driving the debate and buying the outcome. Citizens could pull the levers in the voting booth, but someone with money was pulling the strings behind closed doors.

Democracy in Peril

I

Back in the 1950s, when I first tasted politics and journalism, Republicans briefly controlled the White House and Congress. With the exception of Joseph McCarthy and his vicious ilk, they were a reasonable lot, presided over by the giant war hero Dwight Eisenhower, who was conservative by temperament and moderate in the use of power. That brand of Republican is gone, replaced by zealous ideologues, and for the first time in the memory of anyone alive, the entire federal government—the Congress, the executive, the judiciary—is united behind a right-wing agenda for which George W. Bush believes he now has a mandate.

That includes the power of the state to force pregnant women to give up control over their own lives, the use of the taxing power to transfer wealth to the rich, and the use of the authority of law to give corporations a free hand to eviscerate the environment as well as to control the regulatory agencies meant to hold them accountable. This new hegemony also means secrecy on a scale you cannot imagine and, above all, judges with a political agenda appointed for life. If you liked the Supreme Court that put George W. Bush in the White House, you will swoon over what's coming.

And if you like God in government, get ready for the Rapture. The quasi-theocratic vision of the religious pillars of the new conservative movement is embodied in Tom DeLay, the House majority leader, who has said the Almighty is using him to promote "a biblical worldview" in American politics.

It is indeed a heady time in Washington for piety, profits, and military power, all joined at the hip to ideology and money. Don't forget the money. It came pouring into this election, to both parties, from corporate America and wealthy individuals who will now get back their investment in the form of a disproportionate share of tax cuts, subsidies, and other spoils of victory. Republicans outraised Democrats by $184 million and came up with the big prize—control of the American government and the power of the state to turn their ideology into the law of the land.

Quite a bargain at any price.

—*November 2002*

II

There was a news report in Washington the other day about how Democrats and Republicans in Congress conspired to close down the investigation of an alleged abuse of power by a leading member of the House. Now we'll never know the truth of the matter. The story reminded me of a conversation I had many years ago with a constitutional scholar who said the most important function of one political party is to keep the other party honest. "No party investigates itself," he said, "so the public safety depends on each party shining the spotlight of scrutiny on the shenanigans of the other."

There was a time when the parties could be counted on to mock the deceit, hypocrisy, and pretensions of the opposition, even as they cloaked their own vices in the warm pieties of patriotism and altruism. They also challenged one another's belief systems with the two-fisted ferocity of street brawlers. Such spirited partisanship wasn't a pretty sight for children, but it offered choices, got the public's attention, and aroused a robust and sometimes ribald participation in democracy. Politics mattered.

Things have changed. Republicans still love a good brawl. They will claw, scratch, jam their knee to your groin, and land an uppercut to the jaw after the bell has rung, and if they don't finish the job, their partisan press will do it for them: Rush Limbaugh and the Darth Vaders of talk radio, the righteous pamphleteers at the *Wall Street Journal,* Fox News, and a host of publications aided by big business.

Where are the Democrats? As the Republicans were coming back from the wilderness—lean, mean, and hungry—Democrats were busy assimilating their opponents' belief system. In no small part because they coveted the same corporate money, Democrats practically walked away from the politics of struggle, leaving millions of working people with no one to fight for them. We see the consequences all around us in what a friend of mine calls "a suffocating consensus." Even as poverty increases, inequality grows, and our quality of life diminishes, Democrats have become the doves of class warfare.

Then there's the other war that's coming. Whether you are for or against it, invading Iraq is a diversion of resources and a huge distraction from what ails us. But Democrats signed a blank check over to the president in the fall of 2002 because their leaders wanted "to move on to more important things," namely, the midterm elections, which they lost anyway.

Now Democrats in Congress are so deeply divided and impotent that Ralph Nader is thinking of running again. Maybe third parties will eventually invigorate politics, but what I wouldn't give for a revival of that old-time religion, when both major parties locked horns with the devil—that is, with each other. An Irishman once asked, "Is this a private fight or can anyone get in it?" Democrats should crawl back in the ring and duke it out. Who knows? They might even save the Republicans from themselves.

—March 2003

Here's an example. The Environmental Protection Agency (EPA) estimates that its proposed revisions in air pollution standards for ozone (smog) and fine particles (soot) will lead to 60,000 fewer cases of chronic bronchitis, 250,000 fewer cases of aggravated asthma in children and adults, 1.5 million fewer cases of significant breathing problems, and 20,000 saved lives. Asthma alone is the leading serious chronic illness of children in the United States and the number one cause of school absences attributed to chronic illness. Asthma attacks send an estimated 1.6 million Americans to emergency rooms each year and account for approximately one in six of all pediatric emergency room visits in the United States. The direct health costs from asthma are $9.8 billion per year.

In the Utah Valley near Provo, for example, a researcher from Brigham Young University studied hospital admissions over a period of several years during which a local steel mill closed and then reopened. It was the source of nearly all the small particles on the local atmosphere, and this is an area where, due to the influence of the Mormon Church, fewer people smoke. The study found that the reopening of the mill coincided with a doubling and even tripling (depending on the time of the year) of hospital admissions for pneumonia, pleurisy, bronchitis, and asthma, especially among young people.

Despite this kind of evidence, industry and its beneficiaries, especially right-wing allies, argue that we have already done enough to improve the nation's air. Not suprisingly, the Alliance of Automobile Manufacturers, the American Petroleum Institute, American Electric Power, the National Mining Association, and the National Association of Manufacturers, among others, forged a coalition to fight new air quality standards with a pool of some $30 million in its war chest. The American Lung Association, by comparison, doesn't even have a political action committee.

Nevertheless, despite the intensity of the oppositions, the EPA stood firm, and President Clinton showed some real backbone. In the House of Representatives, however, 192 members signed on to legislation to force the EPA to delay the new standards for at least four years. These members of Congress have received nearly three times as much in campaign contributions from big air polluters than members who did not support the bill. According to the Environmental Working Group, the more money a House member receives from major air polluters, the more likely that politician is to support anti-clean-air legislation. By comparison, representing constituents who live in a heavily polluted area does not necessarily lead a House member to oppose the bill. The money matters more—something to keep in mind when a pundit says that money doesn't buy votes, that our representatives are more influenced by their constituents than their contributors. As one Washington journalist put it, "Soot and smog are not the only pollutants in the air of Capitol Hill. There is also money—so much you can almost breathe it."

Was there ever a time in American history when the elite didn't marshal their resources to protect their privileges? No. Remember Mark Hanna! What's different today is the velocity of the money race, spiraling out of control, overwhelming the political process, leaving people betrayed, angry, and alienated. There is a faint glimmer of hope in the fact that every time voters have had a chance to choose a different way of financing campaigns, they have spoken loud and clear. Sixteen states have adopted reforms in the past three years, and in every state where a reform initiative was on the ballot last year, it passed. While the political class scoffs at the notion that ordinary citizens really care, out across the country a different story is unfolding. The basic idea is clean money. Candidates who voluntarily agree to raise no private money and abide by spending limits, and can demonstrate that they have a basic level of support in their district, can opt to receive clean money from a public fund. This won't end the power of organized special interests in Washington, but with it candidates will have a fighting chance to run serious campaigns. The inherent conflicts of interest that arise when public servants are privately financed will be eliminated, restoring needed public confidence in the process. At a minimum, the voters will finally have a real choice on Election Day.

Some people say this kind of public financing for elections will never fly, that the public won't pay for it, but in fact by one estimate it would only cost about $5 per average taxpayer to cover all congressional elections. That's a small price to pay for cleaning up our elections when you consider how we are now literally paying for hundreds of billions of dollars in boondoggles, special tax breaks, targeted subsidies, and unnecessary spending that result from our privately financed campaign system. *Money* magazine— hardly a socialist organ—estimates that each of us pays $1,600 per year as a result of favors granted to corporations and wealthy people whose campaign contributions get the attention of Congress. It doesn't matter which party controls Congress; the money flows to the top. The rest of us pay.

> We pay at the grocery store. A five-pound bag of sugar costs fifty cents more than it should because year in and year out contributions from the sugar lobby help keep alive sugar price support. An 18-ounce jar of peanut butter costs 33 cents extra because Congress still allows a peanut subsidy.
>
> We pay in higher bills for cable TV service. Because industry poured money into Congress prior to the passage of the Telecommunications Act of 1996, a bill ostensibly aimed to promote competition in the broadcast industry has enabled cable companies to raise their rates at three times the inflation rate since it was passed.
>
> We pay in delays on the release of cheaper, generic drugs, as companies that produce expensive name-brand products use their campaign contributions to obtain from Congress extensions on their monopolies.
>
> We pay for corporate subsidies that conservative Representative

John Kasich estimates cost at least $11 billion per year. (The libertarian Cato Institute suggests the number is closer to $65 billion in unnecessary programs supporting profitable, successful businesses.)

Sometimes people pay with their lives, for actions not taken by government agencies entrusted with protecting our health and safety. Jim Hightower writes of Cynthia Chavez Wall, a single mother who worked at a textile factory near Hamlet, North Carolina, for thirteen years:

She was making eight dollars an hour until she was abruptly fired one day for not coming to work, having stayed home to care for a daughter who had come down with pneumonia. Desperate for a job, she hired on at Imperial Food Products, even though it paid her $4.95 an hour. She cut up and prepared chicken parts that were sold to fast food restaurants. She often went home with her hands bleeding from the cuts she inevitably got trying to keep pace with the constant demands to speed up the process. She worked up against fryers with oil heated to 400 degrees; no air-conditioning, no fans, and only a few small windows. She got thirty minutes for lunch and two fifteen-minute breaks. Complaining about any of this got you nothing but fired, and Ms. Wall had to have a job, so just had to take it.

Then on the morning of September 3, 1991, women in one area of the plant began to yell, "Fire!" Flames flared and smoke billowed throughout the building, which had no sprinkler system, no evacuation plan, and only one fire extinguisher. As the fire spread quickly, panicked workers raced to the exits, but the people shoved on the closed doors to no avail. All but the very front doors had been padlocked from the outside. Company executives later said they did this to prevent chicken parts from being stolen. Trapped, twenty-five of the ninety employees died in the flames. More than fifty others were burned or injured. Cynthia Chavez Wall's body was found at one of the doors.

The media called it a "horrific accident," but as Hightower points out,

> It was no accident. These people were effectively placed in a death trap by their employer—a death trap that had never once in its eleven-year existence been inspected by the U.S. Agriculture Department inspectors checking on the quality of the chicken meat. Earlier in the year the North Carolina legislature had rejected proposals to toughen the state's safety regulation, even though the system is so lax that the average North Carolina workplace is inspected once every seventy-five years. Under Reagan and Bush, Washington, too, had cut back on the number of federal inspectors, leaving us even today with fewer than 1,200 to check out seven million American workplaces.

Then he reminds us that Cynthia Chavez Wall's experience was no anomaly.

> More than 10,000 working people a year (about thirty every single day) die on the job. Ours is the deadliest workplace in the industrialized world. Other industrial nations simply do not put up with such corporate laxity, imposing safeguards that would prevent a majority of death sentences our executives hand down to 10,000 of our people year after year. Two years after Ms. Wall died, two years after the media had scurried away to the next "big story" and the politicians had held their hearings and moved on, a watchdog group called the Government Accountability Project revisited Hamlet and the surrounding area.
>
> Imperial Food Products is no longer there, but the group found that in other poultry plants, nothing has changed. Assembly-line speedups continue to cause excessive injuries, stifling heat and oppressive working conditions remain, ill and injured employees are forced to stay on the line or be fired, and, yes, doors are still locked from the outside.

Rarely do we hear such stories in mainstream media. Instead, we are saturated in coverage of the political merry-go-round in election years at the expense of reports on those behind-the-scene decisions that distribute the spoils of victory to those who have paid to play. No wonder the larger problems facing our nation—increasing job insecurity, declining real wages and income, the shrinking middle class, impoverished children, inadequate and increasingly costly health insurance, a growing disparity of income and wealth, pollution and environmental degradation—cannot be seriously addressed by our politicians. To do so would offend their bankrollers, the campaign contributors.

In his best-selling book a few years ago, *Who Will Tell the People: The Betrayal of American Democracy,* William Greider wrote that the hard questions of governance "are questions of how and why some interests are allowed to dominate the government's decision making while others are excluded." These rarely get explained to the public despite the fact that "this is the reality of politics that matters to people in the everyday lives. [Yet] no one can hope to understand what is driving political behavior without grasping the internal facts of governing and asking the kind of gut-level questions that politicians ask themselves in private: 'Who are the *winners* in this matter and who are the *losers*? Who gets the money and who has to *pay*? Who must be heard on this question and who can be *safely ignored*?' "

The Reverend Carrie Bolton has some answers. The state legislature in North Carolina established a commission to look into campaign financing, and Carrie Bolton came to one of the hearings. She listened patiently as one speaker after another addressed the commissioners, and then it was her time. Her head barely reached the microphone, and she spoke softly at first. Then the passion rose, and her words mesmerized her audience. When she finished, they stood and cheered.

This is what Carrie Bolton said:

I was born to a mother and father married to each other, who were sharecroppers, who proceeded to have ten children. I picked cotton, which made some people rich . . . I pulled tobacco . . . I shook peanuts . . . I dug up potatoes and picked cucumbers, and I went to school . . . with enthusiasm. And with great enthusiasm I memorized the preamble to the Constitution of the United States, I learned the Pledge of Allegiance to the flag, and I was inspired to believe that somehow those things symbolized hope for me against any odds that I might come upon.

I am a divorcée, a single-parent divorcée, and I earn enough money to take care of my two children and myself. And I have managed to get a high school diploma, a bachelor's degree, two master's degrees, and do postdoctoral work.

I am energetic. I'm smart. I'm intelligent.

But a snowball would stand a better chance of surviving in hell than I would running for political office in this country, because I have no money. My family has no money. My friends have no money.

Yet I have ideas. I'm strong, I'm powerful [with her right hand she lifts her left wrist]—people can feel my pulse. People who are working, and working hard, can feel what I feel.

But I can't tell them because I don't know how to get the spotlight to tell them.

Because I have no money.

Anyone who believes Carrie Bolton's cry isn't coming from the soul of democracy is living in a rich fool's paradise.

AMERICA FACES what scholar James Davidson Hunter describes as "the never-ending work of democracy": the tedious, hard, perplexing, messy, and seemingly endless task of working through what kind of people we are going to be and what kind of communities we will live in. Politics is the work of democracy, and it encompasses practically everything that we can and must do together: how we educate our children, design our communities and neighborhoods, feed ourselves and dispose of our wastes, care for the sick and elderly and poor, relate to the natural world, entertain and enlighten ourselves, and defend ourselves. It also affects what values we seek to defend, what roles are chosen for us by virtue of our identity, and what roles we create for ourselves.

These fundamental issues are for all of us to address, as free and equal citizens, through the political process, but when public officials are privately financed millions of Americans are left out. Elections are turned into auctions and access to public officials into a commodity available only to the highest bidders: democracy on the auction block. How long will it be before one or both of America's dominant political parties collapses of its own internal corruption? And what happens if the American people, disgusted by the hollowing out of representative democracy and alienated by the performance of both parties, turn away altogether from civic participation?

I said that I got involved in this issue because of my work at the Schumann Foundation, but there are other reasons as well. I want my three grandchildren to grow up in a healthy civil society where their political worth is not measured by their net worth. Furthermore, I read history, and history is instructive. Here is how the historian Plutarch describes the impact of money on the downfall of the Roman republic:

> The abuse of buying and selling votes crept in and money began to play an important part in determining elections. Later on, however, this process of corruption spread to the law courts and to the

army, and finally, even when the sword became enslaved by the power of gold, the republic was subjected to the rule of emperors.

We are creeping toward an oligarchic society where a relative handful of the rich and privileged decide, with their money, who will run, who will win, and how they will govern. I see no way to stop this trend without ending the arms race and establishing a system of campaign financing that reflects the values of fairness, political equality, and government accountability—the soul of democracy.

It won't be easy. The defenders of the present system will fight hard to hold on to their privilege, and they write the rules. Nothing short of an aroused public will change the system. Nothing less than democracy is at stake.

—1997

WEARING THE FLAG

I wore my flag on air tonight. Until now I hadn't thought it necessary to display a little metallic icon of patriotism for everyone to see. It was enough to vote, pay my taxes, perform my civic duties, speak my mind, and do my part to raise our kids to be good Americans, as they are. Sometimes I would offer a small prayer of gratitude that I had been born in a country whose institutions sustained me, whose armed forces protected me, and whose ideals inspired me; I offered my heart's affections in return. It no more occurred to me to flaunt the flag on my chest than it did to pin my mother's picture on my lapel to prove her son's love. Mother knew where I stood; so does my country. I even tuck a valentine in my tax returns on April 15.

So why wear it? Well, I put it on to take it back. The flag's been hijacked and turned into a logo: the trademark of a monopoly on patriotism. On those Sunday morning talk shows, official chests appear adorned with the flag as if it were the Good Housekeeping Seal. During the State of the Union address, did you notice Bush and Cheney wearing the flag? How come? No administration's patriotism is ever in doubt, only its policies, and the flag bestows no immunity from error.

Most galling are all those moralistic ideologues in Washington sporting the flag in their lapels while writing books, running Web sites, and publishing magazines attacking dissenters as un-American. They are people whose ardor for war grows dispropor-tionately to their distance from the fighting. They belong to the same league as those swarms of corporate lobbyists prowling Capitol Hill with flags in their lapels, trolling for tax breaks even as they call for more spending on war.

So I put on the flag as a modest riposte to men with flags in their lapels who shoot missiles from the safety of Washington think tanks, or argue that sacrifice is good as long as they don't have to make it, or approve of bribing governments to join the coalition of the willing. I put it on to remind myself that the flag belongs to the country, not to the government; that one is not un-American to see war—except in self-defense—as a failure of moral imagination, political nerve, and diplomacy. Come to think of it, standing up to your government can mean standing up for your country.

—*February 2003*

Part Three

THE MEDIA

THE MAKING OF A JOURNALIST

My life as a journalist began half a century ago in East Texas when I went to work for the *Marshall News Messenger* on my sixteenth birthday. I loved my time on that paper, revered the publisher, Millard Cope, after whom I named my first son, and relished living in Marshall. The town in the 1950s was having something of a heyday. It had been one of the first two cities in the nation to fluoridate its water, and right around then a study showing that Marshall children's teeth were 57 percent better than the average kid's made national news. There were so many telephones in town that local numbers had to go to five digits. Marshall, it seemed, had everything. The Marshall Garden Club was planting wisteria everywhere. Van Cliburn, an east Texas native, played a concert at the Marshall City Auditorium; he was only fifteen, and eight years away from the spectacular win at the Tchaikovsky International Competition in Moscow that put a little thaw in the Cold War, but he was already being noticed as a young man "with a great future in music." There was high finance and big business: moonshiners were having their greatest boom since before World War II, and in one monster raid eighty-nine stills in Harrison County were shut down and destroyed. The stuff was going for as much as six or eight dollars a gallon.

There was a local echo of the great national obsession of the age. Millard Cope wrote at least three editorials condemning Joseph McCarthy's methods, but Marshall had its own cell of subversives—the Methodists. After *Reader's Digest* published an article exposing "The Pink Fringe of the Methodists," the pastor of a local Methodist church preached a sermon driving home the same point—that the social gospel embraced by the church was communist at heart.

Wiley College, one of two black colleges in town, put on a road show of George Bernard Shaw's *Caesar and Cleopatra*, and the Kiwanis Club sponsored the passion play *Shepherd of the Hills*, with a cast not exactly of thousands, but certainly of scores—including local folk as extras and a camel brought in from heaven knows where; my brother James, who also worked on the paper, wrote a review singling out the evening's Judas for "one of the most sincere performances of the night." I still have one of the first stories I wrote. It was about a former Marshall woman who was finally reunited with her children nearly half a century after they had been kidnaped by her estranged husband. She fainted when she first heard the news, but then, recovering, she sent a special-delivery letter to her son. Teardrops dotted the pages, I noted.

I moved on eventually, first to North Texas State, where I had a job that would pay my tuition, room, and board, then to Austin, where Lady Bird and LBJ hired me to work at KTBC for $100 a week, enabling me to get married and finish up at the University of Texas. We were the first station in Texas to buy a station wagon, paint it red, and christen it—what else?—Red Rover, so that I could wheel around town in style, broadcasting from crime scenes and accidents and the state legislature, which some people said was the biggest crime scene in town. At the same time I was chasing fire engines for KTBC, I was also following, with a good deal of admiration and some envy, the great fight by my friend Willie

Morris against the regents of the university. Willie had had the brass to write editorials about state politics and its "twin deities, oil and gas," and was hauled in several times for tense chats over menthol cigarettes with the university's president, Logan Wilson. When that gentle persuasion didn't do the trick, the regents "erupted" and imposed a censorship edict on the paper. "The *Texan*," one regent declared, "has gone out of bounds in discussing issues pertaining to oil and gas because 66 percent of Texas tax money comes from oil and gas." At least he was being open about his sacred cows—more than you can say about some news organizations these days—but Willie wouldn't stand for it. He telephoned legendary folklorist J. Frank Dobie to ask for a letter commenting on the issues. "Hell," said Dobie, "I been working' on one all mornin'." The letter was duly sent in and pointed out gently, "The Board of Regents are as much concerned with free intellectual enterprise as a razorback sow would be with Keats's 'Ode on a Grecian Urn.'" That sentence was cut after Willie went home to bed.

After Austin, I kept moving. My path led me on to graduate school, a detour through seminary, then to LBJ's side in Washington, and from there, through circumstances so convoluted I still haven't figured them out, back to journalism, first at *Newsday*, and then the big leap from print to television, to PBS and CBS and back again—just one more of those vagrant journalistic souls who, intoxicated with the moment is always looking for the next high: the lead not yet written, the picture not yet taken, the story not yet told.

It's been a good life. Journalism has been a continuing course in adult education—my own. It enabled me to cover the summits of world leaders and the daily lives of Newark families. I was paid richly as a CBS news analyst to put in my two cents' worth on just about anything that had happened that day. When I made documentaries, I could put in at least a couple of quarters' worth, exploring everything from the power of money in politics to how to make a poem. Journalism provided me a passport into the world of ideas, which became my favorite beat. I've enjoyed the occasionally intimidating privilege of talking to some of the wisest and sanest people around—to philosophers and physicists, novelists and activists, doctors who comfort the old and teachers who inspire the young. I've had the chance to ask them some of the most important questions in the world: why is there something instead of nothing? What do we mean by a moral life? Can we learn to be creative? And one of my favorite questions: what does it mean to be a Texan? I most recently put that question to the sainted writer and activist John Henry Faulk in the last interview he gave before his death in 1990. He told me the story of how he and his friend Boots Cooper were playing in the chicken house when they were about twelve years old. They spied a chicken snake in the top tier of nests, so close it looked like a boa constrictor. As John Henry told it to me, "All our frontier courage drained out our heels— actually it trickled down our overall legs—and Boots and I made a new door through the henhouse wall." His momma came out and, learning what all the fuss was about, said to Boots and John Henry: "Don't you know chicken snakes are harmless? They can't hurt you." And Boots, rubbing his forehead and behind at the same time, said, "Yes, Mrs. Faulk, I know that, but they can scare you so bad, it'll cause you to hurt yourself." John Henry Faulk told me that's a lesson he never forgot. I hope I never do, either.

I've had a wonderful life, matriculating as a perpetual student in the school of journalism. Other people have paid the tuition and travel, and I've never really had to grow up and get a day job. I think it's because journalism has been so good to me that I am also sad when my colleagues and I discuss the state of our craft today and find ourselves debating whether, if we were turning sixteen now, we would again choose to become journalists. We've even debated whether we can in good faith urge young people today to go into journalism at all.

I don't say this easily or lightly. It's painful to talk grumpily about the craft that has been my life for just about two-thirds of all my days, but it is impossible to ignore the fact that celebrity is one of the engines that drives most of what now passes for journalism. If I had to pick out one news story that for me best sums up the decade of the 1990s, it wouldn't be any of the obvious ones: the white Bronco chase, the stained Gap dress, the crash in the Paris underpass, or Matt Drudge on the columnist who doesn't really beat his wife after all. No, it's a brief item that went out over the Associated Press wire about four years back, datelined Santa Monica, California. Here's the lead, exactly as written: "Michael Jackson's plastic surgeon jumped into the ocean to save a suicidal man early today as Hollywood madam Heidi Fleiss called 911 for help." I thought this was a joke at first—something the editors of a college satire magazine might have cooked up—but then I read on:

> Michael Jackson's plastic surgeon jumped into the ocean to save a suicidal man early today as Hollywood Madam Heidi Fleiss called 911 for help. An unidentified 40-year-old man handcuffed himself and jumped a pier just after midnight in this coastal city west of Los Angeles, police said. Dr. Steve Hoefflin, Jackson's surgeon, leaped in after him and kept the man afloat (police said). Fleiss and Dr. Bruce Hensel, a reporter with KNBC, called police. The department keeps a rescue boat at the pier and officers were able to pull both men to safety.

Four people are mentioned in the lead. One—the pop star Michael Jackson, who rates the first two words of the entire story—had absolutely nothing to do with the episode and wasn't even at the scene, but his plastic surgeon happened to be attending a party nearby that was also attended by Heidi Fleiss, the Holly-wood prostitute who herself became a celebrity when she was convicted of running a call girl ring that catered to the rich and famous and whose life then became the subject of a made-for-television movie. She is just a bystander in this story, and all she does is punch in three digits on her telephone, but, like Michael Jackson, she gets her name mentioned because she is famous—or infamous—and further down in the story she gets an entire paragraph devoted to a recap of her career as procuress to the stars, which also has nothing to do with the event on the waterfront. That's not all: believe it or not, the man who leaped in to pull off the rescue—the hero of the piece—doesn't even get his own name into the lead, and wholly lost in the shuffle is the real protagonist of the story, the poor man down there in the water, the victim himself, who isn't identified at all! We're told only that he had been "despondent over his financial state" and was taken to a hospital for psychiatric observation. Just one more hapless Joe whose story wouldn't even matter to the media at all unless it could somehow be tied to our culture's obsession for celebrities.

This reminds of an observation by that old curmudgeon George Bernard Shaw, who said that journalists "are unable, seemingly, to distinguish between a bicycle accident and the collapse of civilization." These days journalists are quite capable of making the distinction, but what they care about is who's having the accident.

It's the latest version of an old game called Trivial Pursuit, aided and abetted today by the wedding of modern technology to media competition in celebrity journalism. A broadcast news executive I admire lost his position because he held up the CBS News report on the crash that killed the Princess of Wales; all he wanted to do was verify it. After all, the first reports from many of the other news organizations said that Diana was fine, she just had a broken arm. When I heard of my friend's fate, I wondered: would it really have mattered to us to wait seven hours to learn that Diana was dead? This kind of thing cost one journalist his job, but what is it costing journalism?

Speed is God today. The CEO of the Associated Press said recently that his organization had been able to transmit the full text of the Starr report over the wires in six seconds flat. In the Watergate era, he said, the same text would have taken thirty-three hours to transmit. Since six seconds is about the same amount of time it took Sam Donaldson to conclude, on his first Sunday morning broadcast after the scandal broke, that Clinton would be done within a week, it seems to me that the Starr report is one text we all could have used an extra thirty-two hours and fifty-four seconds to actually read through, to digest, to ponder, before we all started bloviating about what it meant for the presidency, the country, and the national moral fiber. The airwaves and the news columns are now filled with argument, conflict, chatter, speculation, opinion, prediction, gossip, and brawl, all of which are much cheaper, quicker, and easier to produce than the painstakingly gathered, scrupulously checked, meticulously edited journalism of fact: the increasingly old-fashioned kind of work that actually tells people things they need to know. We celebrate lung power today, not shoe leather.

All these trends—to celebrity journalism, speed over accuracy, opinion over reporting—are part of a larger dynamic that is changing journalism: the concentration of ownership in the hands of megacorporations making megamergers in search of megaprofits. Most recently it was the coupling of Time Warner and AOL—the biggest corporate merger of all time. The media's coverage was agog with gee-whiz reaction and nonstop speculation, but as the cultural critic Todd Gitlin wrote later, the merger was not motivated by any impulse to improve news reporting, magazine journalism, or the quality of public discussion. Its purpose was to boost the customer base, the shareholders' stock, and the executives' personal wealth. Not only is this brave new combination, in Gitlin's words, "unlikely to arrest the slickening of news coverage, its pulverization into ever more streamlined and simple-minded snippers, its love affair with celebrities and show business," the deal is likely to accelerate those trends, since the bottom line "usually abhors whatever is more demanding and complex, slower, more prone to ideas, more challenging to complacency."

The announcement of AOL Time Warner followed by only a few months Viacom's $37-plus-billion marriage to CBS, which topped Disney's $18 billion purchase of ABC, which in turn out-did Time Inc.'s $15 billion acquisition of Warner Communications. Tucked in there somewhere was also the story of an acquisition by NBC, owned by General Electric, that moved it one step toward eventually taking control of another seventy-two television stations, owned by Paxson Communications, which together reach 76 percent of the country. The big fish swallow the small fish, and in turn are swallowed by whales. Today, just six companies dominate what America reads in books, magazines, and newspapers and watches on television and at the movies.

What difference does this make to the average citizen? For one thing, these conglomerates are interested in profits, not journalism. It is more profitable to cover celebrity lifestyles, murder and mayhem, natural disasters, plane crashes, and crime stories than to investigate who is polluting the river, who is getting away with the tax breaks, and what's happening to education. As the conglomeration of ownership gathered steam from 1990 to 1996, the number of crime stories on the network news tripled. One recent study reported that in fifty-five markets in thirty-five states, local news was dominated by crime and violence, triviality and celebrity, and that some stations, in order to feed the bottom line of the media giants that own them, devoted more airtime to commercials than to news. You find the same pattern in newspapers, where the concentration of ownership in local monopolies that are part of large national chains has led to fatter bottom lines at the expense of journalism about what really matters to people's lives. It's the fashion everywhere. I'd say the biggest change in my fifty years in journalism—apart, obviously, from all the technology—has been the shift of content from news about government to consumer-driven information and celebrity features. A study by the Project for Excellence in Journalism, reporting on the front pages of the *New York Times* and the *Los Angeles Times,* on the ABC, CBS, and NBC nightly news programs, and in *Time* and *Newsweek,* showed that from 1977 to 1997 the number of stories about government dropped from one in three to one in five, while the number of stories about celebrities rose from one in every fifty stories to one in every fourteen. Again, what difference does it make? Well, it's government that can pick our pockets, slap us in jail, run a highway through our garden, or send us to war. The veteran journalist Richard Reeves was once asked by a college student to define "real news," and Richard answered: "The news you and I need to keep our freedoms."

What happens when media conglomerates use their control over journalism to promote and protect their own interests? What if they pull their punches on news they don't want covered? We learned after the fact that CBS News balked at blowing the whistle on Big Tobacco because their bosses were afraid of incurring an expensive lawsuit at a delicate time in a merger negotiation, and that the brass at ABC News pulled a segment critical of safety practices at Disney World (although they didn't seem to mind when the people on *Good Morning America* all but donned party hats to travel to Orlando for the theme park's twenty-fifth anniversary). We learned that Rupert Murdoch, desperate to exploit the huge potential market of Chinese consumers, was delighted to have his publishing company issue a fawning biography of Deng Xiaoping by the dictator's own daughter but personally quashed a book by the former governor of Hong Kong that might hurt the Chinese government's feelings.

I don't mean to imply that before the big media conglomerates came along there was some journalistic nirvana. Despite the joy I experienced in my beginnings with the *Marshall News Messenger,* there was a troubling side to both the job and the town that not even a starry-eyed cub reporter could eventually fail to see. The local stories I recounted earlier all concerned white people, even though half the town was black. Only white people counted in those days; only their doings were considered newsworthy. What blacks did, felt, and thought never made the paper. Not even when *Pinky* came to town. *Pinky* stirred a storm across the racist South with its story of a young black woman who passed herself off as white to keep her young white lover. Never mind that it was produced by Darryl Zanuck, directed by Elia Kazan, and starred Jeanne Craine, Ethel Barrymore, and Ethel Waters in performances that won each of them an Oscar nomination. When *Pinky* came to Marshall the town fathers were outraged. Years before, a community censorship board had been established to cope with the racial controversy surrounding *Birth of a Nation.* Now Marshall's leading figures wanted the board resurrected to prevent the showing of *Pinky.* The manager of the Paramount Theatre defied them and was arrested. I don't remember how the episode finally played out, but I know we didn't ask the black folks in town for their views on the subject. For all practical purposes the staff of the paper pretended half of Marshall didn't exist. If blacks got into the paper, it was the same way they got into the movies—through the side door.

I thought of this years later during a summer trip to Ireland, where I learned of an Irish king named Congal who ruled in the early seventh century. A swarm of bees had stung him nearly blind, and when Congal became overking of his clan, he promptly changed Irish law to make bee attacks criminal. He became Congal Caech, which means "Congal the Half-Blind" or "Congal the Squinting, as in Marshall circa 1950.

Even so, it was, as I said, a good place for a kid to learn the trade. Although we squinted at the town around us, the paper had something then that the overkings of the press nowadays seem to have lost: a sense of the mundane webs of ordinary life, the sounds of the human voice in day-to-day transactions of a community. I was originally hired at the paper to follow the stories of the boys who had been drafted to fight the Korean War—boys barely older than I, who had studied with the same teachers as I had and listened to the same radio thrillers, whose peril overseas I too might share if the war lasted until I turned eighteen. I was amazed at how the townspeople lapped up those routine stories I wrote; it was the minute particular, I realized, that fashioned the web of life in a town such as Marshall, and connected those who stayed at home with those who went far off to fight. Journalism narrowed the distance. No cosmic order is offended by the trivialization of journalism, perhaps, but it seems to me that our preoccupation with celebrities today comes at the expense of ordinary people who go about unheralded chores.

I think of Max and Georgiana Lale. Max and I worked together on the paper. As a young reporter in Oklahoma, making $15 a week, he used to sit in his car and listen to the rantings of Adolf Hitler over the radio, hardly knowing that he would one day be in the American army that pushed from Normandy to the Rhine in the crusade to bring Hitler's demonic dreams to an end. When Max came home he returned to newspapering, eventually became a small-town publisher, nourished a lifelong affair with history, and in retirement was elected president of both the Texas State Historical Association and the East Texas Historical Association. When he finally allowed the publication of the letters he wrote home from the battlefield to his young wife, Georgiana, he gave them the simple title *My War.* Max taught me something important about the singular prism through which an individual experiences events, the meaning of which we journalists strive, often unsuccessfully, to understand.

When Georgiana Lale died, I was the commentator on the *CBS Evening News with Dan Rather,* and that night I devoted my two minutes of airtime to her. Hardly anyone outside Marshall— with its population of some twenty thousand people—knew her, of course, but I talked about her community work, her contributions to the church, her feeding of the hummingbirds, and I concluded,

> I cannot count the ways she mattered, or her kind everywhere. If you look closely at the fabric of civilization which overlays the passions of this race, you will discover it held together with tiny rows of thread stitched by the hands of anonymous folk. No community makes it without them; no school, no church, no neighborhood or society. They hold their loyalties with an integrity stronger than any gale but death. Anonymous? Yes. Except to those of us who know them.

That simple little tribute brought thousands of letters pouring into CBS. One came from a truck driver who was listening on his rig's radio and drove two hundred miles out of his way just to visit where this woman had lived. The people who wrote obviously didn't know Georgiana Lale, but they knew someone just like her, they said, and they were grateful that a great network such as CBS had acknowledged to a wider world their presence and their significance.

When I revisit such letters, I know that I have to take back the ambivalence that I admitted earlier. If a sixteen-year-old were to come to me today and say, "Should I go into journalism?" I wouldn't have the heart to say no. I would tell her, though, not to squint—to see the world with both eyes open, so that the Max and Georgiana Lales of the world get their due. I would also tell her about *Pinky* and how half our town was missing on our beat. And I would impress upon her a line from the news photographer in Tom Stoppard's play *Night and Day:* "People do terrible things to each other, but it's worse in places where everybody is kept in the dark."

—2000

JOURNALISM AND DEMOCRACY

When I look back at the twists and turns in my life I still puzzle at the unexpected and unwanted detour I took through the Office of the White House Press Secretary. The first time the president asked me to be his spokesman, I declined. I said that I wanted to return to my post as deputy director of the Peace Corps, from which I had taken leave when the assassination of John Kennedy thrust LBJ into the presidency, or to keep working on domestic policy and legislation from my corner office in the White House. He asked me again, and again I declined. The third time he didn't ask. My arm still hurts.

That night, I told my wife that "this is the beginning of the end." "Why?" she asked. "Because no man can serve two masters," I answered. Less than two years later I was gone.

It took me a while to get my footing back in journalism. I had to learn all over again that what's important for the journalist is not how close you are to power but how close you are to reality. I would find that reality in assignment after assignment, from covering famine in Africa and war in Central America to covering inner-city families trapped in Newark and middle-class families downsized in Milwaukee.

I also had to relearn one of journalism's basic lessons. The job of trying to tell the truth about people whose job it is to hide the truth is almost as complicated and difficult as trying to hide it in the first place. Unless you're willing to fight and refight the same battles until you go blue in the face, drive the people you work with nuts going over every last detail to make certain you've got it right, and then take hit after unfair hit accusing you of "bias," or these days even a point of view, there's no use even trying. You have to love it, and I do.

When I collaborated with the producer Sherry Jones on the very first documentary ever about the purchase of government favors by political action committees, we unfurled across the Capitol grounds yard after yard of computer printouts listing campaign contributions to every member of Congress. That program infuriated just about everyone, including members who had been allies just a few years earlier when I worked at the White House. Congressmen friendly to public television were also outraged, but PBS took the heat without melting.

When we reported the truth behind the Iran-contra scandal for a documentary called *High Crimes and Misdemeanors,* the right-wing posse in town went running indignantly to congressional defenders of lawlessness, and public television again found itself accused of committing—horrors!—*journalism.* We heard from the Clinton White House after a documentary entitled *Washington's Other Scandal,* which exposed the unbridled and illegal fundraising by Democrats in 1996.

But taking on political scandal is nothing compared to what can happen if you raise questions about corporate power in Washington. When my colleague Marty Koughan and I started looking into the subject of pesticides and food for a *Frontline* documentary, Marty learned that industry was attempting behind closed doors to dilute the findings of a National Academy of Sciences study on the effects of pesticide residues on children. Before we finished the documentary, the industry somehow purloined a copy of our draft script—we still aren't certain how—and mounted a sophisticated and expensive campaign to discredit our broadcast before it aired. Television reviewers and the editorial pages of key newspapers were flooded with propaganda. There was a whispering campaign. A *Washington Post* columnist took a dig at the broadcast on the morning of the day it aired—without even having seen it— and later confessed to me that the dirt had been supplied by a top lobbyist for the chemical industry. Some public television managers were so unnerved by the blitz of misleading information about a film they had not yet broadcast that they actually protested to PBS with letters that had been prepared by the industry.

Here's what most perplexed us: eight days before the broadcast, the American Cancer Society—an organization that in no way figured in our story—sent to its three thousand local chapters a "critique" of the unfinished documentary claiming, wrongly, that it exaggerated the dangers of pesticides in food. We were puzzled. Why was the American Cancer Society taking the unusual step of criticizing a documentary that it had not seen, that had not aired, and that did not claim what the society alleged? An enterprising reporter in town named Sheila Kaplan later looked into these questions for *Legal Times*. It turns out that the Porter Novelli public relations firm, which had worked for several chemical companies, also did pro bono work for the American Cancer Society. Kaplan found that the firm was able to cash in some of the goodwill from that "charitable" work to persuade the compliant communications staff at the Society to distribute some harsh talking points about the documentary—talking points that had been supplied by, but not attributed to, Porter Novelli. *Legal Times* headlined the story "Porter Novelli Plays All Sides." A familiar Washington game.

Others also used the American Cancer Society's good name in

efforts to tarnish the journalism before it aired, none more invidi-
ously than the right-wing polemicist Reed Irvine. His screed
against what he called "junk science on PBS" demanded Congress pull the plug on public broadcasting. PBS stood firm. The
documentary aired, the journalism held up, and the publicity lib-
erated the National Academy of Sciences to release the study that
the industry had tried to cripple.

There's always another round, however; the sharks keep cir-
cling. Sherry Jones and I spent more than a year working on
another PBS documentary called *Trade Secrets,* a two-hour investigative special based on revelations—found in the industry's own
archives—that big chemical companies had deliberately withheld
from workers and consumers damaging information about toxic
chemicals in their products. These internal industry documents
are a fact. They exist. They are not a matter of opinion or point of
view. They state what the companies knew, when they knew it,
and what they did with what they knew.

The revelations portrayed deep and pervasive corruption in a
major American industry and raised profound policy implications. We live under a regulatory system designed, it turns out, by
the industry itself. If the public and government regulators had
known what the industry knew about the health risks of its products when industry knew it, America's laws and regulations governing chemical manufacturing would be far more protective of
human health than they are today. But the industry didn't want us
to know. That's the message of the documents and the subject of
our film, and it is the story the industry didn't want us to tell.

The industry hired as an ally a public relations firm in Washington noted for using private detectives and former CIA, FBI, and
drug enforcement officers to conduct investigations for corporations. One of the founders of the company is on record as saying
that sometimes corporations need to resort to unconventional re-

sources, some of which "include using deceit." Given the scurrilous underground campaign that was conducted to smear our journalism, his comments were an understatement. To complicate matters, the single biggest recipient of campaign contributions from the chemical industry over the past twenty years in the House of Representatives is the very member of Congress whose committee has jurisdiction over public broadcasting's appropriations. We didn't use any public funds to produce the documentary, but that didn't stop the pressure that was brought to bear on PBS brass for allowing the program to air. Their stand was vindicated a year later when the National Academy of Television Arts and Sciences awarded *Trade Secrets* an Emmy for outstanding investigative journalism.

Such pressures are nothing, of course, compared to the realities that face journalists elsewhere. Around the world assassins have learned that they can kill reporters with impunity. Journalists are hunted down and murdered because of their reporting—thirty-four in Colombia alone over the past decade. By contrast, America is a utopia for journalists. Don Hewitt, the creator of *60 Minutes,* said to me recently that "the 1990s were a terrible time for journalism in this country but a wonderful time for journalists; we're living like Jack Welch," the CEO of General Electric. Perhaps that's why we aren't asking tough questions of Jack Welch.

I have been lucky. If PBS hasn't flinched when the subjects of our journalism struck back, neither have my corporate underwriter, Mutual of America Life Insurance Company, or my major foundation supporter, the John D. and Catherine T. MacArthur Foundation. The president of the foundation, John Corbally, sought me out as I was leaving CBS to set up an independent production company. The foundation, he said, wanted to encourage "the conversation of democracy" and to encourage debate on public issues. That was fifteen years ago. A dozen years ago the chairman of Mutual of America, William Flynn, also came to see me. His company believed in strong journalism and wanted to become my sole corporate underwriter. I was flabbergasted. Over the years I had lost three corporate funders who had been happy as long as our work didn't make anyone else unhappy. Losing your underwriting, especially when you are an independent producer for public broadcasting, can keep the yellow light of caution flickering in a journalist's unconscious. With the endorsement of Bill Flynn and his successor, Tom Moran, I've never had to think twice about the flickering light, even when reporting controversial stories at the intersection where corporate influence touches political power.

I should declare a bias here. It's one I keep raising: I believe the power of money in politics has tipped the balance against our democratic institutions. Theodore Roosevelt is my mentor on this. TR believed the central fact of his era was that big business had become so dominant it would chew up democracy and spit it out. The power of corporations, he said, had to be balanced with the interest of the general public. Otherwise, America would undergo a class war, the rich would win it, and we wouldn't recognize our country anymore. I believe that is happening. Mighty corporations are again the undisputed overlords of politics and government, their influence permeating the White House, Congress, and, increasingly, the judiciary. At times it seems as if the Business Roundtable, the National Association of Manufacturers, and the American Petroleum Institute function as a super–board of directors for the nation's government, with those secret meetings between Vice President Cheney and executives and lobbyists from oil, gas, and coal companies as an executive committee.

What's the role of journalism in this? The founders of our nation were pretty explicit on this point. The First Amendment is the first for a reason: to hold our representatives accountable and to arm the powerless with the information they need to protect themselves against the tyranny of the privileged elite, whether political or economic. The Founders, however, didn't count on the rise of megamedia. They didn't count on huge private corporations that would own not only the means of journalism but also vast swaths of the terrain that journalism should be covering, including the nexus between economic and political power. According to a recent study by the Pew Research Center for the People and the Press, more than a quarter of journalists polled said they had avoided some newsworthy stories that might conflict with the financial interests of their news organizations or advertisers. It is no coincidence that the news departments of the major broadcast and cable channels virtually blacked out coverage of the 1996 Telecommunications Act, which bestowed enormous new booty on those same media companies.

I became a fanatic—at least a public nuisance—on this issue because of my experience growing up as a southerner and serving in the Johnson White House during the early stages of the Vietnam War. The truth about slavery was driven from the pulpits, newsrooms, and classrooms of the antebellum South; it took a bloody civil war to bring the truth home. Then the truth about Jim Crow was censored, and it took another hundred years to produce the justice that should have followed Appomattox. In the Johnson White House we circled the wagons and grew intolerant of news that didn't conform to our hopes, expectations, and plans, and the results were tragic for America and Vietnam.

I don't want to claim too much for our craft, but I don't want to claim too little, either. One of my journalistic heroes is Martha Gellhorn, who spent half a century observing war and politicians—and journalists, too. By the end she had lost her faith that journalism could, by itself, change the world, but she had found a different sort of comfort. For journalists, she said, "victory and defeat are both passing moments. There is no end; there are only means. Journalism is a means, and I now think that the act of keeping the record straight is valuable in itself. Serious, careful, honest journalism is essential, not because it is a guiding light but because it is a form of honorable behavior, involving the reporter and the reader."

And, one hopes, the viewer, too.

—2001

COUNTERING
THE BASTARD MUSES

I must be the luckiest man in television for having been a part of the public broadcasting community for over half my life. I was present at the creation. As a thirty-year-old White House policy assistant in 1964, I attended the first meeting at the Office of Education to discuss the potential of "educational television," which in turn led to the Public Broadcasting Act of 1967. When I left the White House that year to become publisher of *Newsday* I volunteered for fund-raising chores for Channel Thirteen in New York and appeared on its local newscasts. Then in 1971, through a series of serendipitous events, I came to public television as the correspondent and anchor for a new series called *This Week*.

Now, a quarter of a century and hundreds of broadcasts later—from *Essay on Watergate* to *Amazing Grace,* from *Creativity* and *A Walk Through the Twentieth Century* to *Six Great Ideas with Mortimer Adler* and *Joseph Campbell and the Power of Myth,* from *All Our Children* to *The Language of Life,* from *The Secret Government* to *The Wisdom of Faith* and *Genesis*—I am mindful of what William Temple meant when he said that a person whose life is given to a purpose big enough "to claim the allegiance of all his faculties and rich enough to exercise them is the nearest approach in human experience to the realization of eternity." Public television has provided me such moments, as well as colleagues and kindred spirits who have inspired and nurtured my aspirations—from Fred Rogers and Big Bird to Fred Wiseman, Ken Burns, Robert Mc-Neil, Julia Child, David Fanning, and scores of others. I am just one fish among many in the ocean of public television. This is a big, sprawling, polymorphic community: on our best days an extended family, on our worst days a dysfunctional one. Right now, however, we're facing some hard choices.

- Competitive forces are razing the landscape around us and turf wars are breaking out as they once did between sheepherders and cattlemen.
- Funds for new programming are hard to come by.
- Fevered agents of an angry ideology wage war on all things public—public art, public schools, public libraries, public lands, public health, public parks, and public broadcasting.

All this tumult swirls around a public television community that if not divided is certainly not wholly united in sympathy and aspiration. That's nothing new. In the first speech I made to the Friends of Channel Thirteen back in 1969, I found myself recalling how George Washington had described the new United States of America created by the Constitutional Convention: "It was for a long time doubtful whether we were to survive as an independent republic, or decline . . . into insignificant and withered fragments of empire." The same could be said of public television. From the womb we seemed offspring of the Hatfields and McCoys.

There is no unanimity today on how public television should respond to the rapid changes occurring in telecommunications; there are differences among us over governance; we don't see eye to eye on the mission and role of PBS, station representation in the decision-making process, the responsibilities of membership, the balance between local and national, or the question of back-end rights; we can't even agree on what constitutes core programming. Anyone who proposes solutions for public television winds up with critics on all points of the compass. Perhaps it's the nature of things; a creative community is no respecter of conformity. But I know that the ultimate measure of any system, any society, or any institution is not how it acts in moments of comfort and convenience but how it responds to challenge and controversy.

The best thing we have going for us is a strong and consistent constituency. Somerset Maugham once said, "It is a funny thing about life: if you refuse to accept anything but the best, you very often get it." Millions of Americans look to us for the best that television can deliver, and even when we let them down they seem to keep the faith and grant us a second chance. Deep down the public harbors an intuitive understanding that for all the flaws of public television, our fundamental assumptions come down on their side, and on the side of democracy.

What are those assumptions?

- That public television is an open classroom for people who believe in life-long learning
- That the medium can dignify life instead of debase it
- That it can help us to see more clearly, understand more deeply, and laugh more joyously
- That human creativity combined with technology can provide us with a fuller awareness of the wonder and the variety of the arts and sciences, of scholarship and craftsmanship and innovation, of politics and government and economics and religion and all those mutual endeavors that shape our consciousness
- That commercial broadcasting, having made its peace with "the little lies and fantasies that are the by-products of the mer-

chandising process," is too firmly fixed within the rules of the economic game to rise more than occasionally above the lowest common denominator

- That Americans are citizens and not just consumers, and (in the words of the educator Herbert Kohl) "if we do not provide time for the consideration of people and events in depth, we may end up training another generation of TV adults who know what kind of toilet paper to buy, who know how to argue and humiliate others, but who are thoroughly incapable of discussing, much less dealing with, the major social and economic problems that are tearing America apart"

Those of us who helped launch public television were not disdainful of commercial television. We ourselves turned to it for news, diversion, and amusement. We knew that it helped to keep the economy dynamic through the satisfaction or creation of appetites. We are a capitalist society, after all. The market is a cornucopia of goods and services, and television programs are part of that market. There is always something to sell, and television can sell. But public television was meant to do what the market will not do. From the outset we believed there should be one channel not only free of commercials but free from commercial values; a channel that does not represent an economic exploitation of life; a channel whose purpose is not to please as many consumers as possible, in order to get as much advertising as possible, in order to sell as many products as possible; a channel—at least one—whose success is measured not by the numbers who watch but by the imprint left on those who do.

Considered the report delivered to the PBS Board of Directors a while back by Gale Metzger of Statistical Research. He found that:

- When people look for a program on science or the arts, or a program their children can watch, they look first to public television.
- We rated higher with people who want to understand issues that are important to society.
- Two-thirds of the people see our news and public affairs as a mixture of political persuasions—they think we are fair.
- As for the charge of elitism, public television rated about the same with people who have a high school education or less as it did with people who have a college degree or higher.
- Eighty percent of the people even think that on-air pledge drives are a fair price to pay for the programming they get from public television.
- Most important, two out of three people said it would make a difference to their lives if public television did not exist.

Now that's the statistical reassurance. But if it's not enough, I take to the streets to learn all over again what our mission is about. A letter came just last week from a man named Bart Shutzbank. He is an inmate at a prison near Philadelphia, and he wrote how much his life has been touched by the people he has met through public television. Even now he has been watching—for the second time—my series with Huston Smith, *The Wisdom of Faith*. It has helped him, he said, "to keep the divine spark alive inside these walls."

I had a letter last week from a retired truck driver who lives in San Lorenzo, California. He had seen the recent *Frontline* documentary on middle-class Americans living on the edge in a downsized economy, and it confirmed what he had witnessed on a trip of forty-seven hundred miles through fourteen states. He found that "the city streets and back roads tell stories of poverty that are glossed over on the newscasts." He had written letters to several major newspapers to call attention to what he had seen, but none was printed, and he wanted to thank public television for reporting that was true to experience.

A few years ago we produced a series about contemporary American poets, *The Power of the Word*. We included well-known poets such as Stanley Kunitz, Quincy Troupe, Galway Kinell, Sharon Olds, Robert Bly, and W.S. Merwin as well as emerging poets like Li-Young Lee, Joy Harjo, and James Autry. Our cameras followed them to readings at locations as varied as a New York prison, a high school and a bar in St. Louis, a church in rural Mississippi, a meeting of business executives in Iowa, and two poetry festivals. Thousands of people wrote in response to that series.

From a woman in Georgia:

I'm not in the habit of writing at all, much less for a television series, but the series may have changed all that. What a glimpse of the soul those programs gave us. After watching [the first one] I felt pleased all the next day about being human. The programs have a universal appeal, as though they have tapped into some plan that everyone can experience. My eleven-year-old, horse-riding, Nintendo junkie of a child does not move an inch when the series is on. We never suggested she watch with us; somehow she magically appears, watches in silence, and leaves in silence. I can see she's been touched, and we have no need to discuss anything about the series. It's just there. Perhaps that's what poetry is about, and I thank you.

From a college professor:

This past semester, at my chairman's urging, I offered a seminar on *The Power of the Word* to eleven junior and senior English majors, seven of whom presently plan to become teachers themselves. There were two men and nine women, ranging in age from twenty-one to forty-one. Several were married; two had children already in school. As a group, my class was probably typical of public college students.

Because they were insecure about poetry, not uncommon even for English majors, and because this was my first extended experience with *The Power of the Word* in the classroom and *also* my first experience of continuously teaching without working from the printed page, we all began the semester with more than normal apprehension. In fact, as they became more assured and more trusting, they confided that throughout the semester they began watching each program warily and usually felt connected to each new group of poets and poems only after class discussion *and* a second viewing.

I think all this animal suspicion derives from the cultural conditioning that has prepared us for disappointment and frustration when directly encountering poetry. Happily, for these students the actual experience of poetry consistently and universally led to pleasure, delight, and greatly strengthened self-confidence. . . .

But let me tell you about just one of these students. Jean is in her early thirties, married, and she has three children—the youngest was only two months old when we began the course in September. I had taught her before and had always found her energetic but anxious and somehow doomed to reduce all experience to a formula. She had taken a different junior-level seminar with another teacher last year, had done poorly, and was taking this seminar with me only because she needed a higher grade in this required course to graduate. She came to the screening of the first program with a bad head cold, and she snuffled and snorted so steadily throughout that I barely restrained my impulse to ask her to step outside so the others could watch and listen undistracted. Fortunately, something stayed my tongue and the criticism it carried, but I left the class convinced that she would somehow bring all my hopes for the class to ruin. This was Thursday, and she had signed up to take responsibility for opening the discussion of this first program on the following Tuesday.

On Tuesday she seemed almost another person. . . . She began by describing her experience of the previous week's in-class screening, never mentioning her cold; she only described how frightened and confused she had been. She took the cassette home and watched it on Thursday night and again on Friday night without feeling any closer to the poets or to the poems. Then on Saturday morning she woke up, looked out the window, saw a tree in leaf under the blue sky and suddenly felt "reborn to poetry." . . . She said, "When I watched the program on Friday evening, I *thought* I felt it, but when I watched it again on Saturday morning I *really* felt it." The face of this woman, whom I had almost written off, literally glowed as she proudly declared, again, that she had been "reborn to poetry."

Because such a breakthrough was exactly what I had always hoped the program could accomplish, I had trouble accepting that it was in fact really happening here and now. Only when the rest of the class enthusiastically followed her lead and, as if on cue, each offered similar testimony of the program's success in touching his or her inner life was I finally brought to accept our triumph for what it clearly was. Poetry seems such a simple answer to our confusion and to our inability to see either clearly or deeply.

Here is another of my favorites, this one from a high school teacher in New Jersey:

This is a letter from the trenches. I don't think of teaching English as "being in the trenches," but . . . when I met you briefly after the reception for *The Power of the Word* and mentioned I was a high school teacher, you . . . said something about the trenches.

I teach four classes—two sophomore composition classes, a junior general English course (which our school dubs a noncollege preparatory course, as if to cancel those kids out), and a poetry class. So far this year, I have used at least two of the segments in all the classes and all six segments in the poetry class. (We are lucky in our school to have a one-semester poetry course—an oddity.)

I thought you might be interested in how *The Power of the Word* played. First, Alfie and Quincy Troupe. Alfie's not exactly your high-powered intellectual; in fact, he hasn't had too much use for poetry until Quincy Troupe appeared on the screen. Now he's writing in his journal, "I'm starting to like poetry." There are at least three more Alfies in the junior general English of sixteen students—all starting to like poetry. (Most of the rest, by the way, have been closet poets, so your series brought a lot of their work out in the open.)

In fact, everyone really liked Quincy Troupe. Of all the poets in the series, he was the one that inspired audience participation in the classroom—shouts, "right, man," "yo," repetition of his lines with him—which is not surprising unless you know I teach in an all-white school . . . where, regrettably, there is still a lot of racial prejudice. Many students wrote that they admired Troupe for going into the prison to teach. One class wanted to see the prison segment again and again—they were partly fascinated by the "madman poem," but they were interested too in Troupe's comments about dehumanization. . . . When the packing house poem was over, half the class could quote lines from it. With my general English students—where prejudice against minorities is strongest—Troupe gave an opening to introduce other black poets. . . . (Many high school students, by the way, still have that primal love for rhyme and rhythm, so when [Langston] Hughes says, rejecting suicide, "life is fine, fine as wine, life is fine," they remember it.)

Second, Jennifer and [poet] Sharon Olds. Jennifer, like Alfie, is also in my junior general class. After we watched the first segment of *The Power of the Word,* we read some more of Sharon Old's poetry: "The Abandoned Newborn" and "The Blue Dress." Jennifer really liked the fact the Olds was, as she said, so "honest" and that she could "talk about her body." At least twenty-five young girls loved Olds. She seemed especially important to students—male and female—whose parents had been divorced. She was talking for them and their pain.

Third, there's Sean and Sharon Olds. Sean, like several of my other young men in general English, was initially shocked by Sharon Olds. They seemed to feel "private things and how did her husband feel." When I told the students they could try writing a Sharon Olds poem, most of them imitated "The Abandoned Newborn" and wrote about what they saw on TV that night—the San Francisco Earthquake. However, Sean wrote what . . . most people would call a sado-masochistic description of a woman's torture and rape. We spent a long time then in class talking about the difference between erotic and pornographic literature, between lovers as equals and man/woman relationships when one has power and the other is a victim. It was an important discussion. After the discussion Sean, at least, did understand, because he stayed after class, and told me that after thinking about it, he had decided to tear up the poem. He had no idea how the women in the class would feel about what he had written.

I could write another ten pages of examples. But since I have to return to the trenches tomorrow morning, I will summarize. Your series permitted student after student to write and say things that they could not have written or said before. Each student found a poet to whom to connect—though some loved Merwin and others disliked him, some liked Bly and others didn't. From reading the journals that students shared with me, I thought that none went away empty. The series fed their spirits. It permitted us to say things that we would not have said.

I think teaching is an act of faith, rather than an act of warfare. Making TV programs must be even more of an act of faith. Thank you very much for your series—you and all the people who helped you put it together. The word does become flesh.

During the bicentennial of the Constitution in 1987 my associates and I produced a PBS series on the Constitution in contemporary life. Several members of the Supreme Court participated as well as legal scholars, historians, philosophers, and regular citizens whose defense of their First Amendment rights had taken them all the way to the highest court in the land. Among the letters we received was one from a housewife in a western state:

I have never written a letter like this before. I am a full-time wife and mother of four children under seven years and I am entirely busy with the ordinary things of family life. However, I want to thank you very much for *In Search of the Constitution*. As a result of this series, I am awakened to a deep appreciation of many ideals vital to our democracy. I am much moved by the experience of listening at the feet of thoughtful citizens, justices, and philosophers of substance. All these are people with whom I will never converse on my own, and I am grateful to you for having brought these conversations within my sphere. I am aware that I lack eloquence to express the measure of my heart's gratitude. I can say, however, that these programs are a landmark among my life's experiences. Among all the things I must teach my children, a healthy interest in understanding the Constitution now ranks very prominently. Thank you.

Then there is *Joseph Campbell and the Power of Myth*. It premiered in the summer, with not a cent of promotion, to a minuscule rating. It went on to be one of the most successful series in public television's history, repeated many times and seen by millions upon millions of viewers And it started as a mere leap of faith. What drew me to him? He was a man with a thousand stories, this was one of his favorites. In Japan for an international conference on religion, Campbell overheard another American delegate, a social philosopher from New York, say to a Shinto priest, "We've been now to a good many ceremonies and have seen quite a few of your shrines. But I don't get your ideology. I don't get your theology." The Japanese paused as though in deep thought and then slowly shook his head. "I think we don't have ideology," he said. "We don't have theology. We dance." And so did Joseph Campbell—to the music of the spheres.

Among those millions touched by the series was a young woman in her mid-thirties who stopped me in midtown Manhattan and wanted to tell me her story. She had come to New York eight years earlier to make her way as an actress. The breaks were fugitive: someone else always got the part. Her boyfriend of many years left her for another woman. Her father died. She was broke and working as a waitress to make ends meet. She decided life was no longer worth living. Disenchanted and defeated, she went home one evening—she pointed to her studio apartment, across the street from where we were standing—and she pulled down the window, poured a glass full of bourbon, turned on the gas burners of her stove, lay down on the couch, and prepared for the curtain to fall. But the television set was on. She heard two fellows talking about the experience of being alive; and her ears perked up. She listened intently, and when the program ended and the announcer said, "Be sure to join us next week as we continue our conversation with Joseph Campbell," she decided she wanted to be around for it. She got up from the couch, turned off the gas, poured her drink into the sink, and opened the window. "I realized at that moment," she said, "I don't have to be an actress, but I do want to be alive. I want to experience my life—every minute of it."

Then there are the cab drivers: Youssef Jaoa, for one. He came to New York from Morocco six years ago. He was studying hotel management when we talked a year ago, and he told me he would be getting his degree this spring. Youssef kept his car radio tuned to National Public Radio all day and his television set at home on Channel Thirteen. He said, "I am blessed by these stations." He pointed at a picture on the dashboard of his thirteen-month-old son, and he said, "My son was born in this country. I will let him watch public television so he can learn how to be an American."

Shouldn't public television aspire to be the core curriculum of the American experience? E.D. Hirsch in *Cultural Literacy: What Every American Needs to Know* lamented that our schools no longer are teaching young people the essential ingredients of a general education. He told of the high school teacher who mentioned to his students that Latin is a dead language, no longer spoken. One girl raised her hand to challenge his claim. If Latin is a dead language, she wanted to know, "what do they speak in Latin America?" Hirsch made the case that cultural literacy is far more than a skill; it requires certain essential knowledge if we are to function effectively in the world and collaborate in society. "To grasp the words on a page," he said, "we have to know a lot of information that isn't on the page." He called this knowledge "cultural literacy" and described it as "that network of information all competent readers possess." It's what enables us to read a book or an article with an adequate level of comprehension, getting the point, grasping the implications, reaching conclusions: our common information. Some people criticized Hirsch on the grounds that teaching the traditional literature culture means teaching elitist information. That is an illusion, he says. Literature culture is the most democratic culture in our land: it excludes nobody; it cuts across generations and social groups and classes; it's what every American needs to know, not only because knowing it is a good thing but also because other people know it too.

This was the Founders' idea of an informed citizenry: that people in a democracy can be entrusted to decide all-important matters for themselves because they can communicate and deliberate with one another. "Economic issues can be discussed in public. The moral dilemmas of new medical knowledge can be weighed. The broad implications of technological change can become subjects of informed public disclosure," writes Hirsch. We might even begin to understand how—and for whom—politics really works. For example, early last year we produced a special on money and politics. We showed how private money continues to drive public policy and how our campaigns have become auctions instead of elections. As the broadcast came to a close, we put on the screen the 800 number of a nonpartisan group called Project Vote Smart. When you call the number they send you a printout showing the campaign donors to every representative in Congress. In response to that one broadcast, almost thirty thousand Americans got up from their chairs and couches, went over to their phones, and dialed the number!

But informing citizens is not all we're about.

Americans are assaulted on every front today by what the scholar Cleanth Brooks called "the bastard muses":

- *Propaganda,* which pleads, sometimes unscrupulously, for a special cause at the expense of the total truth
- *Sentimentality,* which works up emotional responses unwarranted by and in excess of the occasion
- *Pornography,* which focuses on one powerful drive at the expense of the total human personality

Newsweek recently reported on "the appalling accretion" of violent entertainment that "permeates Americans' life—an unprecedented flood of mass-produced and mass-consumed carnage masquerading as amusement and threatening to erode the psychological and moral boundary between real life and make-believe."

How do we counter it? Not with censorship, which is always counterproductive in a democracy, but with an alternative strategy of affirmation. Public broadcasting is part of that strategy. We are free to regard human beings as more than mere appetites and America as more than an economic machine. Leo Strauss once wrote, "Liberal education is liberation from vulgarity." He reminded us that the Greek word for vulgarity is *apeirokalia,* the lack of experience in things beautiful. A liberal education supplies us with that experience and nurtures the moral imagination. I believe a liberal education is what we're about. Performing arts, good conversation, history, travel, nature, critical documentaries, public affairs, children's programs—at their best they open us to other lives and other realms of knowing.

The ancient Israelites had a word for it: *hochma,* the science of the heart. Intelligence, feeling, and perception combine to inform your own story, to draw others into a shared narrative, and to make of our experience here together a victory of the deepest moral feeling of sympathy, understanding, and affection. This is the moral imagination that opens us to the reality of other people's lives. When Lear cried out on the heath to Gloucester, "You see how this world goes," Gloucester, who was blind, answered, "I see it feelingly." When we succeed in helping people see the world this way, the public square is a little less polluted, a little less vulgar, and our common habitat a little more hospitable. That is why we must keep trying our best. There are people waiting to give us an hour of their life—an hour they never get back—provided we give them something of value in return. We are engaged in a moral transaction. Henry Thoreau got it right: "To affect the quality of the day, is the highest of the arts."

—1991, 1996

THE FIGHT OF OUR LIVES

More and more thoughtful journalists—and citizens in general—are embracing the cause of media reform. I must confess, however, to a certain discomfort, shared with other journalists, about the very term *media*. Ted Gup, who teaches journalism at Case Western Reserve, articulated my concerns when he wrote in *The Chronicle of Higher Education* (November 23, 2001),

> The very concept of media is insulting to some of us within the press who find ourselves lumped in with so many disparate elements, as if everyone with a pen, a microphone, a camera, or just a loud voice were all one and the same. . . . David Broder is not Matt Drudge. "Meet the Press" is not "Temptation Island." And I am not Jerry Springer. I do not speak for him. He does not speak for me. Yet "the media" speaks for us all.

That's how I felt when I saw Oliver North reporting on Fox from Iraq, pressing our embattled troops to respond to his repetitive and belittling question, "Does Fox rock? Does Fox rock?" Oliver North and I may be in the same media, but we are not part of the same message. Nonetheless, I accept that I work and all of us live in medialand, and God knows we need some media reform. But those two words—*media reform*—are really an incomplete description of the job ahead. Taken alone, they suggest that we're a bunch of efficiency experts, tightening the bolts and boosting the output of the machinery of public enlightenment, or else a conclave of high-minded do-gooders applauding each other's sermons. But we need to be—and we will be—much more than that. Because what we're talking about is nothing less than rescuing a democracy that is so polarized it is in danger of being paralyzed and pulverized.

Those are alarming words, granted, but the realities we face should trigger alarms. Free and responsible government by popular consent can't exist without an informed public. That's a cliché, I know, but I agree with the presidential candidate who once said that truisms are true and clichés mean what they say (an observation that no doubt helped to lose him the election). Democracy can't exist without an informed public. For example, only 13 percent of eligible young people cast ballots in the last presidential election. A recent National Youth Survey revealed that only half of the fifteen hundred young people polled believe that voting is important, and only 46 percent think they can make a difference in solving community problems: fully 25 percent of the electorate. The Carnegie Corporation conducted a youth challenge quiz of fifteen- to twenty-four-year-olds and asked them, "Why don't more young people vote or get involved?" Of the nearly two thousand respondents, the main answer was that they did not have enough information about issues and candidates. So it's not simply the cause of journalism that's at stake today, but the cause of American liberty itself. As Tom Paine put it, "The sun never shined on a cause of greater worth." He was talking about the cause of a revolutionary America in 1776. But that revolution ran in good part on the energies of a rambunctious though tiny press.

Freedom and freedom of communications were birth twins in the future United States. They grew up together, and neither has fared very well in the other's absence. Boom times for the one have been boom times for the other.

Yet today, despite plenty of lip service on every ritual occasion to freedom of the press, radio and TV, three powerful forces are undermining that very freedom, damming the streams of significant public interest news that irrigate and nourish the flowering of self-determination. The first of these is the centuries-old reluctance of governments—even elected governments—to operate in the sunshine of disclosure and criticism. The second is more subtle and more recent: the tendency of media giants, operating on big-business principles, to exalt commercial values at the expense of democratic value—that is, to run at full throttle what Edward R. Murrow forty-five years ago called broadcasting's "money-making machine." In so doing they are squeezing out the journalism that tries to get as close as possible to the verifiable truth; they are isolating serious coverage of public affairs into ever-dwindling "news holes," far from prime time; and they are gobbling up small and independent publications competing for the attention of the American people.

It's hardly a new or surprising story. But there are fresh and disturbing chapters. In earlier times our governing bodies tried to squelch journalistic freedom with the blunt instruments of the law—padlocks for the presses and jail cells for outspoken editors and writers. Over time, with spectacular wartime exceptions, the courts and the Constitution struck those weapons out of their hands. But they've found new ones now, in the name of "national security." The classifier's Top Secret stamp, used indiscriminately, is as potent a silencer as a writ of arrest. And beyond what is officially labeled "secret" there hovers a culture of sealed official lips, opened only to favored media insiders: a culture of government

by leak and innuendo and spin, of misnamed "public information" offices that churn out blizzards of releases filled with self-
justifying exaggerations and, occasionally, just plain damned lies.
It's censorship without officially appointed censors.

Add to that the censorship-by-omission of consolidated media
empires digesting the bones of swallowed independents, and
you've got a major shrinkage of the crucial information upon
which thinking citizens can act. People saw that coming as long as
a century ago when the rise of chain newspaper ownerships, and
then of concentration in the young radio industry, became apparent. And so in the zesty progressivism of early New Deal days, the
Federal Communications Act of 1934 was passed. The aim of that
cornerstone of broadcast policy, mentioned over a hundred times
in its pages, was to promote the "public interest, convenience and
necessity." The clear intent was to prevent a monopoly of commercial values from overwhelming democratic values: to ensure
that the official view of reality—corporate or government—was
not the only view of reality that reached the people. Regulators
and regulated, media and government were to keep a wary eye on
each other, preserving the checks and balances that are the bul-
wark of our constitutional order.

What would happen, however, if the contending giants of big
government and big publishing and broadcasting ever joined
hands, ever saw eye to eye in putting the public's need for news
second to free-market economics? That's exactly what's happening now under the ideological banner of "deregulation." Giant
media conglomerates that our founders could not possibly have
envisioned are finding common cause with an imperial state in a
betrothal certain to produce not the sons and daughters of liberty
but the very kind of bastards that issued from the old arranged
marriage of church and state.

Consider the situation. Never has there been an administration

Public Access in Peril

Lyndon Johnson signed the Freedom of Information Act (FOIA) on July 4, 1966. He signed it, he said in language that was almost lyrical, "with a deep sense of pride that the United States is an open society in which the people's right to know is cherished and guarded." Well, yes, but as his press secretary at the time, I knew something that few others did: LBJ had to be dragged kicking and screaming to the signing ceremony. He hated the very idea of the Freedom of Information Act, hated the thought of journalists rummaging in government closets, hated them challenging the official view of reality. He dug in his heels and even threatened to pocket-veto the bill after it reached the White House. Only the courage and political skill of a congressman named John Moss got the bill passed at all, and that was after a twelve-year battle against his elders in Congress, who blinked every time the sun shined in the dark corridors of power. They managed to cripple the bill Moss had drafted, and even then only some last-minute calls to LBJ from a handful of newspaper editors overcame the president's reluctance. He signed "the f——thing," as he called it, and then went out to claim credit for it.

It's always a fight to find out what the government doesn't want us to know, a fight we're once again losing. Not only has George W. Bush eviscerated the Presidential Records Act and FOIA, he has clamped a lid on public access across the board. In response, historians and other scholars have joined with public interest groups to challenge in court the Bush executive order limiting access to presidential records. It's not just historians and journalists the administration wants locked out, however, it's Congress, it's you: the public and its representatives.

We're told it's for national security, but keeping us from finding out about the possibility of accidents at chemical plants is not about national security, it's about covering up an industry's indiscretions. Locking up the secrets of meetings with energy executives is not about national security, it's about hiding the confidential memorandum sent to the White House by Exxon Mobil showing the influence of oil companies on the administration's policy on global warming. We only learned about that memo, by the way, thanks to the Freedom of Information Act.

The government's obsession with secrecy is all the more disturbing because the war on terrorism is a war without limits, without a visible enemy or decisive encounters. We don't know what's going on, how much it's costing, where it's being fought, and whether it's effective. That gives a handful of people enormous power to keep us in the dark, and it justifies other abuses. Vice President Cheney continues to lead the fight to keep Americans from knowing what their government knew about terrorist threats before September 11. He also still resists our knowing how corporations were allowed to decide the Bush energy policies that handed them billions of dollars in taxpayer subsidies. This is potentially a bigger scandal than the heist of Teapot Dome, which rocked the Harding administration. That one also involved vast amounts of oil. Look it up on the Web. It's no secret.

—*April 2002*

so disciplined in secrecy, so precisely in lockstep in keeping information from the people at large and—in defiance of the Constitution—from their representatives in Congress. Never has the powerful media oligopoly—the word is media mogul Barry Diller's, not mine—been so unabashed in reaching like Caesar for still more wealth and power. Never have hand and glove fitted together so comfortably to manipulate free political debate, sow contempt for the idea of government itself, and trivialize the people's need to know. When journalism throws in with power, the first news marched by censors to the guillotine is the news the authorities don't want us to know. The greatest moments in the

MARKET CONDITION THAT EXISTS WHEN THERE are
few sellers

history of the press came not when journalists made common cause with the state but when they stood fearlessly independent of it.

Which brings me to the third powerful force that is shaping what Americans see, read, and hear: the quasi-official partisan press ideologically linked to an authoritarian administration that in turn is the ally and agent of the most powerful financial interests in the world. This convergence dominates the marketplace of political ideas today in a phenomenon unique in our history. You need not harbor the notion of a vast right-wing conspiracy to think this collusion more than pure coincidence. Conspiracy is unnecessary when ideology hungers for power and its many adherents swarm of their own accord to the same pot of honey. Stretching from the editorial pages of the *Wall Street Journal* to the faux news of Rupert Murdoch's empire to the nattering nabobs of know-nothing radio to a legion of think tanks bought and paid for by conglomerates, the religious, partisan, and corporate right has raised a mighty megaphone for sectarian, economic, and political forces that aim to transform the egalitarian and democratic ideals embodied in our founding documents. With no strong opposition party to challenge such triumphalist hegemony, it is left to journalism to be democracy's best friend. That is why so many journalists and ordinary citizens questioned the bid by Michael Powell, chairman of the Federal Communications Commission (FCC)—and blessed by the White House—to permit further concentration of media ownership. If free and independent journalism committed to telling the truth without fear or favor is suffocated, the oxygen goes out of democracy.

And there is no surer way to intimidate and then silence mainstream journalism than to be the boss. Just read Jane Kramer's chilling account in the *New Yorker* of Silvio Berlusconi. The prime minister of Italy is its richest citizen and its first media mogul. The list of media that he or his relatives or his proxies own, or directly or indirectly control, includes the state television networks and radio stations, three of Italy's four commercial television networks, two big publishing houses, two national newspapers, fifty magazines, the country's largest movie production and distribution company, and a chunk of its Internet services. Even now he is pressing upon parliament a law that would enable him to purchase more media properties, including the most influential paper in the country. Kramer quotes one critic who says that half the reporters in Italy work for Berlusconi, and the other half think they might have to. Small wonder that he has managed to put the Italian state to work to guarantee his fortune—or that his name is commonly attached to such unpleasant things as contempt for the law, conflict of interest, bribery, and money laundering. Nonetheless, writes Kramer, "his power over what other Italians see, read, buy, and, above all, think, is overwhelming." Kramer quotes the editor of *The Economist,* Bill Emmott, as recently asking why a British magazine was devoting so much space to an Italian prime minister. He replied that Berlusconi had betrayed the two things the magazine stood for: capitalism and democracy. Can it happen here? Yes, it can. By the way, Berlusconi's close friend is Rupert Murdoch. On July 31 this year, writes Kramer, programming on nearly all the satellite hookups in Italy was switched automatically to Murdoch's Sky Italia.

So the issues go beyond media reform. It is, in fact, one of the great ongoing struggles of the American experience—the struggle to maintain government "of, by, and for the people." It's a battle we can win only if we work together, as we saw in action a few months ago. The FCC, heavily influenced by lobbyists for the newspaper, broadcasting and cable interests, prepared a relaxation of the rules governing ownership of media outlets that would allow still more diversity-killing mergers among media giants.

The proceedings were conducted in virtual secrecy and generally ignored by all the major media, who were of course interested parties. In June Chairman Powell and his two Republican colleagues on the FCC announced the revised regulations as a done deal.

But they didn't count on the voice of independent journalists and citizens. Because of coverage in independent outlets—including PBS, which was the only broadcasting system that encouraged its journalists to report what was really happening—and because citizens took quick action, this largely invisible issue burst out as a major political cause and ignited a crackling public debate. Powell was exposed for his failure to conduct an open discussion of the rule changes save for a single hearing in Richmond, Virginia. Quick action by aroused citizens led to a real participatory discussion, with open meetings in Chicago, Seattle, San Francisco, New York, and Atlanta. The organizing that followed generated millions of letters and filings at the FCC opposing the change. Finally, the outcry mobilized unexpected support for bipartisan legislation to reverse the new rules, and the bill cleared the Senate—although House majority leader Tom DeLay still holds it prisoner in the House. But who would have thought six months ago that the cause would win support from such allies as Senator Trent Lott or Kay Bailey Hutchinson, from my own Texas? Media reform has arrived at center stage, where it may even now become a catalyst for a new era of democratic renewal.

We working journalists have something special to bring to this work. We can ably address the mechanics of reform. What laws are needed? What advocacy programs and strategies? How can we protect and extend the reach of the tools that give us some countervailing power against media monopoly—instruments like the Internet, cable TV, community-based radio and public broadcasting systems, alternative journals of news and opinion? But without passion, without a message that has a beating heart, these won't be enough. Here journalism can serve as a true agent of freedom, although not the only one, obviously. In fact, journalism is a deeply human and therefore deeply flawed craft. But at times it has made other freedoms possible. The draftsmen of the First Amendment knew this, and we cannot afford to forget it.

The establishment of press freedom wasn't ordained to protect hucksters, and it didn't drop like gentle rain from heaven. It was fought and sacrificed for by unpretentious but feisty craftsmen who got their hands inky at their own hand presses and called themselves simply "printers." The very first American newspaper was a little three-page affair put out in Boston in September 1690, *Publick Occurrences Both Foreign and Domestick*. The editor, Benjamin Harris, wrote that he simply wanted "to give an account of such considerable things as have come to my attention." The government shut it down after just one issue for the official reason that the printer hadn't applied for the required government license to publish. But I wonder if some Massachusetts notable didn't take personally one of Harris's proclaimed motives for starting the paper: "To cure the spirit of Lying much among us."

No one seems to have objected when Harris and his paper disappeared—that was the way things were. But some forty-odd years later, when printer John Peter Zenger was jailed in New York for criticizing its royal governor, things were different. The colony brought Zenger to trial on a charge of "seditious libel," and since it didn't matter whether the libel was true or not, the case seemed open and shut. But the jury ignored the judge's charge and freed Zenger, not only because the governor was widely disliked, but because of the closing appeal of Zenger's lawyer, Andrew Hamilton. His client's case was

Not the cause of the poor Printer, nor of New York alone, [but] the cause of Liberty, and . . . every Man who prefers Freedom to a Life of Slavery will bless and honour You, as Men who . . . by an impartial and uncorrupt Verdict, [will] have laid a Noble Foundation for securing to ourselves, our Posterity and our Neighbors, That, to which Nature and the Laws of our Country have given us a Right,—the Liberty—both of exposing and opposing arbitrary Power . . . by speaking and writing—Truth.

That is still a good mission statement.

During the War for Independence itself most of the three dozen little weekly newspapers in the colonies took the patriot side and mobilized resistance by giving space to anti-British letters, news of Parliament's latest outrages, and calls to action. But the clarion journalistic voice of the revolution was the onetime editor of the *Pennsylvania Magazine,* Tom Paine, a penniless recent immigrant from England, where he left a trail of failure as a businessman and husband. In 1776—just before enlisting in Washington's army—he published *Common Sense,* a hard-hitting pamphlet that slashed through legalisms and doubts to make an uncompromising case for an independent and republican America. It's been called the first best-seller, with as many as a hundred thousand copies bought by a small literate population. Paine followed it up with another convincing collection of essays written in the field and given another punchy title, *The Crisis.* Passed from hand to hand and reprinted in other papers, they spread the gospel of freedom to thousands of doubters. Paine had something we need to restore—an unwavering concentration to reach ordinary people with the message that they mattered and could stand up for themselves. He couched his gospel of human rights and equality in a popular style that any working writer can envy. "As it is my design," he said, "to make those that can scarcely read understand, I shall therefore avoid every literary ornament and put it in language as plain as the alphabet."

That plain language spun off memorable one-liners that we're still quoting. "These are the times that try men's souls." "Tyranny, like hell, is not easily conquered." "What we obtain too cheap, we esteem too lightly." "Virtue is not hereditary." And this: "Of more worth is one honest man to society and in the sight of God than all the crowned ruffians that ever lived." I don't know what Paine would have thought of political debate by bumper sticker and sound bite, but he could have held his own in any modern campaign.

There were also editors who felt responsible to audiences that would dive deep. In 1787 and 1788 the small *New-York Independent Advertiser* ran all eighty-five numbers of *The Federalist*, those serious essays in favor of ratifying the Constitution. They still shine as clear arguments, but they are, and were, unforgiving in their demand for concentrated attention. Nonetheless, *The Advertiser* felt that it owed the best to its readers, and the readers knew that the issues of self-government deserved their best attention. I pray that media reform may mean a press as conscientious as the *New-York Advertiser*, as pungent as *Common Sense*, and as public-spirited as both. It takes those qualities to fight against the relentless pressure of authority and avarice. In 1791, when the First Amendment was ratified, the idea of a free press seemed safely sheltered in law. It wasn't. Only seven years later, in the midst of a war scare with France, Congress passed and John Adams signed the infamous Sedition Act. It prohibited circulating opinions "tending to induce a belief" that lawmakers might have unconstitutional or repressive motives, or "directly or indirectly tending" to justify France or to "criminate"—whatever that meant—the president or other federal officials. No wonder opponents called it a scheme to "excite a fervor against foreign aggression only to establish tyranny at home." John Ashcroft would have loved it.

But at least a dozen editors refused to be frightened and went defiantly to prison, some under state prosecutions. One of them, Matthew Lyon, who also held a seat in the House of Representatives, languished for four months in an unheated cell during a Vermont winter. But such was the spirit of liberty abroad in the land that admirers chipped in to pay his thousand-dollar fine, and when he emerged his district reelected him by a landslide. Luckily, the Sedition Act had a built-in expiration date of 1801, at which time President Jefferson—who had hated it from the first—pardoned those remaining under indictment. So the story has an upbeat ending, and so can ours, but it will take the kind of courage that those early printers and their readers showed.

Courage is a timeless quality and surfaces when the government is tempted to hit the bottle of censorship again during national emergencies, real or manufactured. In 1971, during the Vietnam War, the Nixon administration resurrected the doctrine of "prior restraint" from the crypt and tried to ban the publication of the Pentagon Papers by the *New York Times* and the *Washington Post,* even though the documents themselves were a classified history of events that occurred during four earlier presidencies. Arthur Sulzberger, the publisher of the *Times,* and Katherine Graham, of the *Washington Post,* were both warned by their lawyers that they and their top managers could face criminal prosecution under espionage laws—or at the least, punitive lawsuits or whatever political reprisals a furious Nixon team could devise—if they printed the material that Daniel Ellsberg had leaked. He had offered the papers without success to the three major television networks, but after internal debates—and the threats of some of their best-known editors to resign rather than fold under pressure—

both newspaper owners gave the green light, and were vindicated by the Supreme Court. Score a round for democracy.

Bipartisan fairness requires me to note that the Carter administration, in 1979, tried to prevent *The Progressive* from running an article called "How to Make an H-Bomb." The grounds were a supposed threat to "national security." But Howard Morland had compiled the piece entirely from sources open to the public, mainly to show that much of the classification system was Wizard of Oz smoke and mirrors. The courts again rejected the government's claim, but it's noteworthy that the journalism of defiance by that time had retreated to a small left-wing publication like *The Progressive,* edited by Erwin Knoll.

In all three of those cases, confronted with a clear and present danger of punishment, none of the owners flinched. Can we think of a single executive of today's big media conglomerates showing the kind of resistance that Sulzberger, Graham, and Erwin Knoll did? Certainly not Michael Eisner: he said he didn't even want ABC News reporting on its parent company, Disney. Certainly not General Electric/NBC's Robert Wright: he took Phil Donahue off MSNBC because the network didn't want to offend conservatives with a liberal sensibility during the invasion of Iraq. Instead, NBC brought to its cable channel one Michael Savage, whose diatribes on radio had described nonwhite countries as "turd-world nations" and who characterized gay men and women as part of "the grand plan to cut down on the white race." I am not sure what it says that the GE/NBC executives calculated that while Donahue was offensive to conservatives, Savage was not.

And then there's Leslie Moonves, the chairman of CBS. In the very week that the once-Tiffany network was celebrating its seventy-fifth anniversary—and taking kudos for its glory days, when it was unafraid to broadcast *The Harvest of Shame* and *The*

Selling of the Pentagon—the network's famous eye blinked. Pressured by a vociferous and relentless right-wing campaign and bullied by the Republican National Committee—at a time when its parent company has billions resting on whether the White House, Congress, and the FCC will allow it to own even more stations than currently permissible—CBS caved in and pulled a miniseries about Ronald Reagan that conservatives thought insufficiently worshipful. Moonves said that taste, not politics, dictated his decision, but earlier this year, explaining why CBS intended to air a series about Adolf Hitler, Moonves sang a different tune: "There are times when as a broadcaster when you take chances." This obviously wasn't one of those times. Granted, made-for-television movies about living figures are about as vital as the wax figures at Madame Tussaud's—and even less authentic; granted that the canonizers of Ronald Reagan hadn't even seen the film before they set to howling; granted, on the surface it's a silly tempest in a teapot. Still, when a once-great network falls obsequiously to the ground at the feet of a partisan mob over a cheesy miniseries that practically no one would have taken seriously as history, you have to wonder if the slight tremor that just ran through the First Amendment could be the harbinger of greater earthquakes to come, when the stakes are really high. And what concessions may the media tycoons-cum-supplicants be making when no one is looking?

So what must we devise to make the media safe for individuals stubborn about protecting freedom and serving the truth? And what do we all—educators, administrators, legislators, and activists—need to do to restore the disappearing diversity of media opinions? America had plenty of that in the early days when the republic and the press were growing up together. It took no great amount of capital and credit—just a few hundred dollars—to start a paper, especially with a little political sponsorship and help. There were well over a thousand of them by 1840, mostly small-town weeklies. And they weren't objective by any stretch.

Here's William Cobbett, another Anglo-American hell-raiser like Paine, shouting his creed in the opening number of his 1790s paper, *Porcupine's Gazette.* "Peter Porcupine," Cobbett's self-bestowed nickname, declared:

> Professions of impartiality I shall make none. They are always use-less, and are besides perfect nonsense, when used by a newsmon-ger; for, he that does not relate news as he finds it, is something worse than partial; and . . . he that does not exercise his own judg-ment, either in admitting or rejecting what is sent him, is a poor passive tool, and not an editor.

In Cobbett's day you could flaunt your partisan banners as you cut and thrust, and not inflict serious damage on open public dis-cussion because there were plenty of competitors. It didn't matter if the local gazette presented the day's events entirely through a Democratic lens. There was always a Whig or Republican alter-native handy—there were, in other words, choices. As Alexis de Tocqueville noted, these many blooming journals kept even rural Americans amazingly well informed. They also made it possible for Americans to exercise one of their most democratic habits—that of forming associations to carry out civic enterprises. And they operated against the dreaded tyranny of the majority by let-ting lonely thinkers know that they had allies elsewhere. Here's how de Tocqueville put it:

> It often happens in democratic countries that many men who have the desire or directed toward that light, and those wandering spirits who had long sought in each other the need to associate

cannot do it, because all being very small and lost in the crowd, they do not see each other and do not know where to find each other. Up comes a newspaper that exposes to their view the sentiment or the idea that had been presented to each of them simultaneously but separately. All are immediately in the shadows finally meet each other and unite.

No wandering spirit could fail to find a voice in print. And so in that pre-Civil War explosion of humanitarian reform movements, it was a diverse press that put the yeast in freedom's ferment. Of course there were plenty of papers that spoke for Indian-haters, immigrant-bashers, bigots, jingoes, and land-grabbers proclaiming America's Manifest Destiny to dominate North America. But one way or another, journalism mattered, and had purpose and direction.

Past and present are never as separate as we think. Horace Greeley, the reform-loving editor of the *New York Tribune,* not only kept his pages "ever open to the plaints of the wronged and suffering" but said that whoever sat in an editor's chair and didn't work to promote human progress hadn't tasted "the luxury" of journalism. I liken that to the words of a kindred spirit closer to our own time, I.F. Stone. In his four-page little *I.F. Stone's Weekly,* Izzy loved to catch the government's lies and contradictions in the government's own official documents. And amid the thunder of battle with the reactionaries, he said: "I have so much fun I ought to be arrested." Here we have two newsmen, a century apart, believing that being in a position to fight the good fight isn't a burden but a lucky break.

That era of a wide-open and crowded newspaper playing field began to fade as the old hand presses gave way to giant machines with press runs and readerships in the hundreds of thousands and costs in the millions. But that didn't necessarily or immediately kill public-spirited journalism, not so long as the new owners were still strong-minded individuals with big professional egos to match their thick pocketbooks. When Joseph Pulitzer, a onetime immigrant reporter for a German-language paper in St. Louis, took over the *New York World* in 1883, he was already a millionaire in the making. But here's his recommended short platform for politicians:

1. Tax Luxuries
2. Tax Inheritances
3. Tax Large Incomes
4. Tax Monopolies
5. Tax the Privileged Corporation
6. A Tariff for Revenue
7. Reform the Civil Service
8. Punish Corrupt Officers
9. Punish Vote Buying.
10. Punish Employers Who Coerce their Employees in Elections

Also not a bad mission statement. What huge newspaper chain today would take that on as an agenda?

The *World* certainly offered people plenty of the spice that they wanted—entertainment, sensation, earthy advice on living—but not at the expense of news that let them know who was on their side against the boodlers and bosses. Nor did big-time, big-town, big-bucks journalism extinguish the possibility of a reform-minded investigative journalism that took the name of muckraking during the Progressive era. Because, in the words of Samuel S. McClure, owner of *McClure's Magazine,* when special interests defied the law and flouted the general welfare, there was a social debt incurred. As he put it: "We have to pay in the end, every one of us. And in the end, the sum total of the debt will be our liberty."

Muckraking lingers on today, but alas, a good deal of it consists of raking personal and sexual scandal in high and celebrated places. If democracy is to be served, we have to get back to putting the rake where the important dirt lies, in the fleecing of the public and the abuse of its faith in good government.

When the landmark Communications Act of 1934 was under consideration, a vigorous public movement of educators, labor officials, and religious and institutional leaders emerged to argue for a broadcast system that would serve the interests of citizens and communities. A movement like that is coming to life again, and we now have to nurture the momentum.

It won't be easy, because the tide's been flowing the other way for a long time. The deregulation pressure began during the Reagan era, when then FCC chairman Mark Fowler, who said that TV didn't need much regulation because it was just a "toaster with pictures," eliminated many public interest rules. That opened the door for networks to cut their news staffs, scuttle their documentary units (goodbye to *The Harvest of Shame* and *The Selling of the Pentagon),* and exile investigative producers and reporters to the underfunded hinterlands of independent production. It was like turning out streetlights on dark and dangerous corners. A crowning achievement of that drive was the Telecommunications Act of 1996, the largest corporate welfare program ever for the most powerful media and entertainment conglomerates in the world—passed, I must add, with support from both parties.

The beat of convergence between once-distinct forms of media goes on at increased tempo, with the communications conglomerates and the advertisers calling the tune. As safeguards to competition fall, an octopus such as GE-NBC-Vivendi-Universal will be able to secure cable channels that can deliver interactive multimedia content—text, sound, and images—to digital TVs, home computers, personal video recorders, and portable wireless devices like cell phones. The goal, as they freely admit, is to corner the market on new ways of selling more things to more people for more hours in the day, and in the long run to fill the airwaves with pitches customized to you and your children. That will melt down the surviving boundaries between editorial and marketing divisions and create a hybrid known to the new-media hucksters as "branded entertainment."

Consider what's happening to newspapers. A study by Mark Cooper of the Consumer Federation of America reports that two-thirds of today's newspaper markets are monopolies. And now most of the country's powerful newspaper chains are lobbying for co-ownership of newspaper and broadcast outlets in the same market, increasing their grip on community after community. In fact, on December 3, 2003, such media giants as the *New York Times,* Gannett, Cox, and Tribune, along with the trade group representing almost all the country's broadcasting stations, filed a petition with the FCC making the case for the cross ownership the owners so desperately seek. They actually told the FCC that lifting the regulation on cross ownership would strengthen local journalism. But did those same news organizations tell their readers what they were doing? Not at all: none of them on that day believed they had an obligation to report in their own news pages what their parent companies were asking of the FCC. As these huge media conglomerates increase their control over what we see, read, and hear, they rarely report on how they themselves are using their power to further their own interests and power as big business, including their influence over the political process.

Then there is the revealing new book *Leaving Readers Behind: The Age of Corporate Newspapering* (published as part of the Project on the State of the American Newspaper under the auspices of the Pew Charitable Trusts). It is the product of people who love newspapers—Gene Roberts, former managing editor of the *New*

York Times, Thomas Kunkel, dean of the Philip Merrill College of Journalism, and Charles Layton, a veteran wire service reporter and news and feature editor at the *Philadelphia Inquirer,* as well as contributors such as Ken Auletta, Geneva Overholser, and Roy Reed. Their conclusion: the newspaper industry is in the middle of the most momentous change in its three-hundred-year history—a change that is diminishing the amount of real news available to the consumer. A generation of relentless corporatization is now culminating in a furious, unprecedented blitz of buying, selling, and consolidating of newspapers, from the mightiest dailies to the humblest weeklies, creating a world.

- Where small hometown dailies in particular are being bought and sold like hog futures
- Where chains, once content to grow one property at a time, now devour other chains whole
- Where the chains are effectively ceding whole regions of the country to one another, further minimizing competition
- Where money is pouring into the business from interests with little knowledge and even less concern about the special obligations newspapers have to democracy.

The authors describe the toll that the never-ending drive for profits is taking on the news. In Cumberland, Maryland, for example, the police reporter had so many duties piled upon him that he no longer had time to go to the police station for the daily reports. But newspaper management had a cost-saving solution: put a fax machine in the police station and let the cops send over the news they thought the paper should have. In New Jersey, the Gannett chain bought the *Asbury Park Press,* then sent in a publisher who slashed fifty-five people from the staff and cut the space for news, and was rewarded by being named Gannett's Manager of the Year. In New Jersey, by the way, the Newhouse and Gannett chains between them now own thirteen of the state's nineteen dailies, or 73 percent of all the circulation of New Jersey–based papers. Then there is the *Northwestern* in Oshkosh, Wisconsin, with a circulation of 23,500, which prided itself on being in hometown hands since the Johnson administration—the Andrew Johnson administration. But in 1998 it was sold not once but twice, within the space of two months. Two years later it was sold again: four owners in less than three years. Indeed, *Leaving Readers Behind* came to the sobering conclusion that the real momentum of consolidation is just beginning; it won't be long now before America is reduced to half a dozen major print conglomerates.

You can see the results even now:

- In the waning of robust journalism
- In the dearth of in-depth reporting as news organizations try to do more with fewer resources
- In the failure of the major news organizations to cover their own corporate deals
- In the scant reporting of lobbying and other forms of "crime in the suites" such as the Enron story

Moreover, newspapers are not helping people understand their government. The report includes a survey in 1999 that showed a wholesale retreat in coverage of nineteen key departments and agencies in Washington. Regular coverage of the Supreme Court and State Department dropped off considerably through the decade. At the Social Security Administration, whose activities literally affect every American, only the *New York Times* was maintaining a full-time reporter. And incredibly, there were no full-time reporters at the Interior Department, which controls five to six hundred million acres of public land and looks after everything from the National Park Service to the Bureau of Indian Affairs.

Out across the country there is simultaneously a near blackout of local politics by broadcasters. The public interest group Alliance for Better Campaigns studied forty-five stations in six cities in one week in October 2003. Out of 7,560 hours of programming analyzed, only 13 were devoted to local public affairs—less than one-half of 1 percent of local programming nationwide. Mayors, town councils, school boards, and civic leaders get no time from broadcasters who have filled their coffers by looting the public airwaves, over which they were placed as stewards. Last year, when a movement sprang up in the House of Representatives to require these broadcasters to obey the law that says they must sell campaign advertising to candidates for office at the lowest commercial rate, the powerful broadcast lobby brought the Congress to heel. So much for the "public interest, convenience, and necessity."

So what do we do? What is our strategy for taking on what seems a hopeless fight for a media system that serves as effectively as it sells—one that holds all the institutions of society, itself included, accountable? Here's one journalist's list of some of the overlapping and connected goals that a vital media reform movement might pursue.

First, we have to take Tom Paine's example and reach out to regular citizens. Those of us concerned about the issue must reach the audience that's not here—carry the fight to radio talk shows, local television, and the letters columns of our newspapers. As Danny Schecter of MediaChannel.org has urged, we must engage the mainstream, not retreat from it. We have to get our fellow citizens to understand that what they see, hear, and read is not only the taste of programmers and producers but also a set of policy decisions made by the people we vote for.

We have to fight to keep the gates to the Internet open to all. The Web has enabled many new voices in our democracy—and globally—to be heard: advocacy groups, artists, individuals, non-profit organizations. Just about anyone can speak online, and often with an impact greater than in the days when orators had to climb on a soapbox in a park. The media industry lobbyists point to the Internet and say that therefore concerns about media concentration are ill founded in an environment where anyone can speak and where there are literally hundreds of competing channels, but they don't divulge the fact that the traffic patterns of the online world are beginning to resemble those of television and radio. In one study, for example, AOL Time Warner (as it was then known) accounted for nearly a third of all user time spent online. And two others companies—Yahoo! and Microsoft—bring that figure to fully 50 percent. As for the growing number of channels available on today's cable systems, most are owned by a small handful of companies. Of the ninety-one major networks that appear on most cable systems, seventy-nine are part of such multiple-network groups such as Time Warner, Viacom, Liberty Media, NBC, and Disney. In order to program a channel on cable today, you must be either owned by or affiliated with one of the giants. If we're not vigilant, the wide-open spaces of the Internet could be transformed into a system in which a handful of companies use their control over high-speed access to ensure they remain at the top of the digital heap in the broadband era at the expense of the democratic potential of this amazing technology. We must fight to make sure the Internet remains open to all as the present-day analogue of that many-tongued world of small newspapers so admired by de Tocqueville.

We must fight for a regulatory, market, and public opinion environment that lets local and community-based content be heard rather than drowned out by nationwide commercial programming.

We must fight to limit conglomerate swallowing of media outlets by sensible limits on multiple and cross ownership of TV and radio stations, newspapers, magazines, publishing companies, and other information sources.

We must fight to expand a noncommercial media system—something made possible in part by the new digital spectrum awarded to PBS stations—and fight off attempts to privatize what's left of public broadcasting. Commercial speech must not be the only free speech in America!

We must fight to create new opportunities, through public policies and private agreements, to let historically marginalized media players into more ownership of channels and control of content.

In the meantime, traditional mainstream journalism must get tougher about keeping a critical eye on those in public and private power and keeping us informed of what's important—not necessarily simple or entertaining or good for the bottom line. Not all news is *Entertainment Tonight*. News departments are trustees of the public, not of the corporate media's stockholders

In that last job, schools of journalism and professional news associations have their work cut out. We need journalism graduates who are not only better informed in a whole spectrum of special fields—and the schools do a competent job there—but who take from their training a strong sense of public service. We also need graduates who are perhaps a little more hard-boiled and street-smart than the present crop, though that's hard to teach. Thanks to the high cost of education, we get very few recruits from the ranks of those who do the world's unglamorous and low-paid work. But

as a onetime "cub" in a very different kind of setting, I cherish
H.L. Mencken's description of what being a young Baltimore reporter a hundred years ago meant to him. "I was at large," he
wrote,

> in a wicked seaport of half a million people with a front seat at
> every public . . . [B]y all orthodox cultural standards I probably
> reached my all-time low, for the heavy reading of my teens had
> been abandoned in favor of life itself. . . . But it would be an exag-
> geration to say I was ignorant, for if I neglected the humanities I
> was meanwhile laying in all the worldly wisdom of a police lieu-
> tenant, a bartender, a shyster lawyer or a midwife.

We need some of that worldly wisdom in our newsrooms.

Professional associations of editors might remember that in
union there is strength. One journalist alone can't extract from an
employer a commitment to let editors and not accountants
choose the appropriate subject matter for coverage. But what if
news councils blew the whistle on shoddy or cowardly manage-
ments? What if foundations gave magazines such as the *Columbia
Journalism Review* sufficient resources to spread their stories of
journalistic bias, failure, or incompetence? What if entire editorial
departments simply refused any longer to quote anonymous
sources, or give Kobe Bryant's trial more than the minimal space it
rates by any reasonable standard, or run stories that are planted by
the Defense Department and impossible, for alleged security reasons, to verify? What if a professional association backed them to
the hilt? Or required the same stance from all its members? It
would take courage to confront powerful ownerships in that way,
but not as much courage as is asked of those brave journalists in
some countries who face the dungeon, the executioner, or the secret assassin for speaking out.

All this may be in the domain of fantasy; then again, maybe not. What I know to be real is that we are in for the fight of our lives. I am not a romantic about democracy or journalism; the writer André Gide may have been right when he said that all things human, given time, go badly. But I know journalism and democracy are deeply linked in whatever chance we have to redress our grievances, renew our politics, and reclaim our revolutionary ideals. Those are difficult tasks at any time, and they are even more difficult in a cynical age such as this, when a deep and pervasive corruption has settled upon the republic. But too much is at stake for our spirits to flag.

Just recently the Library of Congress gave the first Kluge Lifetime Award in the Humanities to the Polish philosopher Leslie Kolakowski. In an interview Kolakowski said: "There is one freedom on which all other liberties depend—and that is freedom of expression, freedom of speech, of print. If this is taken away, no other freedom can exist, or at least it would be soon suppressed." That flame of truth must carry the movement forward. I am getting older and will not be around for the duration. But I take heart from all the people working for a free and independent press, and from the spirit of Peter Zenger, Thomas Paine, the muckrakers, I.F. Stone and those many heroes and heroines, celebrated or forgotten, who faced odds no less than ours and did not flinch.

—2003

Part Four

LOOKING BACK

WHERE THE JACKRABBITS WERE

When I was born in 1934 my father was making $2 a day working on the construction of a new highway from the Texas border to Oklahoma City. We were living in the southeastern corner of Oklahoma in an area known as "Little Dixie" because so many people had come there from Arkansas, Texas, Louisiana, Mississippi, and Alabama.

I have not spent any time in Oklahoma for years, although my childhood impressions were sharply etched in my mind and I have always felt that men like my father, coming to maturity in the 1920s and laid low by the 1930s, were a special lot: they were born before Oklahoma was admitted to the Union, and the state took shape around their labors and losses. They had no option but to cope, and their experiences fueled a whole generation's determination not to repeat them. As Adam Smith wrote a few years ago, "It is the first generation off the farm that provides the longest hours and the most uncomplaining workers." It wasn't sheer ambition alone that drove my crowd in the 1950s to hallow the success ethic; we had memories. I went back last week and the memories were still there. My father, who is seventy now, came up on the bus from Texas, and we drove from Oklahoma City down through familiar parts of the state. His brother, my uncle Harry, still lives in Pauls Valley, an hour south of Oklahoma City; he and Aunt Emily have moved into town from the farm they rented and worked for more than a quarter of a century. Even at sixty-eight, however, Uncle Harry can't stay away from the land; partly to earn money—their old-age assistance is less than $200 a month—and partly from habit, he hires out when someone needs him. "I'd make good wages if I could just find the work," he said. This summer he took a hoe to a hundred acres of soybeans and earned $2.50 an hour, which he says "was a big help to Momma and me when the inflation bug hit." They still grow potatoes, corn, tomatoes, and okra, and at lunch Aunt Emily served strawberry cake and three pies.

A late afternoon sun the size of a prospector's imagination was hanging in the sky as we drove out to their old farm. Along the Washita River is a levee that Uncle Harry built with a team of mules; in those days he and my father and men like them qualified to vote in local elections by helping to build country roads—two days of work to qualify if they brought a mule, five if not. "There was a time during the Depression when the only meat we had to eat was jackrabbits we caught in the fields," my father said. "And sometimes," Uncle Harry added, "we'd run alongside 'em to feel their ribs to see if they were fat enough t'cook." Uncle Harry has never been able to pull a Republican lever when he votes; he always thinks of Herbert Hoover and jackrabbits.

The old house to which Uncle Harry brought Aunt Emily from Little Dixie in 1930 is still standing in the fields a hundred yards from the river, abandoned and beginning to fall apart—a simple frame house with two bedrooms where eight children were born. "I couldn't even afford to buy this land when it was selling for $200 an acre thirty years ago," Uncle Harry said. "Now they're getting $2,000 to $3,000 an acre, not for people to grow things on but for shopping centers and stuff like that." He sighed and said: "Even in the worst times I couldn't leave it. It almost killed Momma and me, but this place needed us as much as we needed it. They got bulldozers now, and it don't need us any-more."

My father and I drove on southeast through an Oklahoma that is changing fast and prospering in complicated ways. But now we were putting the past together again. My father's parents married in Tahlequah, in what was then Indian Territory, and moved south of the Red River into Texas to farm the waxy black land. When grandfather died the family returned to Oklahoma with a new stepfather. They owned four mules and two wagons, a buckboard buggy, two milk cows, two calves, a pig, and some chickens. The January weather was cold and wet, and it took them two days to travel thirty miles. After they had ferried the Red River near Frogville the two young mules got stuck in the muddy bottom land, became excited and scared trying to get out, and turned the wagon over into the muck. My father, who was then twelve, and his brother Harry tried to recover some of Grandmother's canned fruits but failed.

They settled in Choctaw County, not far from where the Trail of Tears had ended years earlier for the Chickasaw, Choctaw, Cherokee, Seminole, and Creek Indians who had been forcefully removed by the U.S. government from their old lands in the Deep South. Sadness and hardship were the lot of most people, red and white, who tried to impose their hope on the realities of nature in this part of the country, and the incident on the Red River was only a harbinger of difficult times to come. Men swore and watched helplessly as it rained when they didn't want it or didn't when they desperately needed it. Their wives cooked on wood-stoves, washed clothes in black pots, buried children who couldn't survive the diphtheria and malaria, and bore more who did; twin daughters born to my mother both died, one of whom might have been saved had there been a doctor or medicine nearby. When flu and pneumonia struck, people wrapped asafet-ida gum in a cloth around the necks of their ailing kin and waited, often in vain.

In the winter they shook with the cold, and in the summer they sweltered. My father and his brother used to scoop fifteen tons of cottonseed a day from a wagon onto a conveyor belt, in 110-degree heat, for 50 cents a ton each. That was a temporary job when the gins were running, and the rest of the time they tried to farm, always on another man's land—fourteen hours a day behind a team of mules. My father wanted to stay in farming but had to give up shortly before I was born. He had expected to get half a bale of cotton to the acre on thirty-five acres, but it rained all of July and half of August and the boll weevils came like an Old Testament plague and it was over; he went to work on the highway. Eventually he got a job driving a truck for a creamery—$15 and expenses for a six-day week—and we moved to Texas. One by one his own brothers—except for Uncle Harry—left the land, migrating to California and into the pages of a Steinbeck novel.

In recapturing the past last week, we were not trying to do so in some idealized way, to make things what they never were, nor to escape; a seventy-year old man who has buried four of his five children doesn't extol the good old days, and I still have places to be. We were looking, instead, for landmarks to share again after years of separate journey, and in ordinary places, while there was still time, we found them.

—*1974*

EMPTY NEST

We did this weekend what many of you have done before us, and many will do yet. We delivered our final-born to his freshman year at college and came home to an empty nest. This was some weekend for news—the Middle East, Mexico, Poland—but it all went right past me. The noise of this world could not compete with the silence of a house where the laughter and tears of children are now only echoes in the mind.

My friend Erma Bombeck has a way with these things that I envy. "One of these days," said Erma, "you'll shout, 'Why don't you kids grow up and act your age?' And they will, and you'll be left to wish for tablecloths stained with spaghetti, for anxious nights with the vaporizer, for PTA meetings, rainy weekends beneath a leaky scout tent, and the tooth fairy adjusted for inflation." These, and not the public's hurrah, suddenly become the measure of a life.

Yet in the *Wall Street Journal* recently an essay described changes in America that have made it ever harder to rear healthy, competent children. So many anchors of stability have been hoisted that a lot of people are deciding against child rearing altogether. I understand their fears and I know the risks; I know there are people who do not have children for very good reasons, but I'm grateful for having been spared a good reason. Without children, I might never have been spared the toxic absorption with myself. I might not have discovered unconditional love. And I might not have discovered how the circles of loyalty that nurture children, from family to schools to civic groups, churches, and the public library, nurture all of us, too, as members of the whole society. So I would not have seen so clearly that these are worth our best efforts for the sake of the children and the sake of the nation.

At a nearby table in a restaurant the other night, I overheard one young couple debating the matter of children: the trials and tribulations, the loss of mobility, the cost in money and emotion—all bound up in the question, "Should we start a family?" Thinking about it this weekend, among the memories of an empty nest, I'm sorry now that I didn't go over to their table and cast an affirmative vote.

—1982

SECOND THOUGHTS

In his old age Reinhold Niebuhr wrote a book to revise his previously held opinions. I can't imagine LBJ doing such a thing, because it would have taken too long for a man who believed that action was the measure of the day, but I think he would have been the first to agree that any estimate of his role in history will require a continuing round of second opinions.

There is no last judgment on a president, only a series of interim reports. This is mine. It is subjective. It is biased, and it is circumscribed by the reality that while Lyndon Johnson was in Washington thirty-one years, I worked for him fewer than four of those years. There are many people who served him longer and more wisely than I. Their portrait of him would be fuller, their judgments sounder, their memories richer. I was present for only three of his campaigns and just over three of the five White House years. But my experiences with him were exhilarating and excruciating.

He was thirteen of the most interesting and difficult men I ever met—at times proud, sensitive, impulsive, flamboyant, sentimental, bold, magnanimous, and graceful (the best dancer in the White House since George Washington); at times temperamental, paranoid, ill of spirit, strangely and darkly uneasy with himself. He owned and operated a ferocious ego, and he had an animal sense of weakness in other men. He could inflict on them a thousand cuts before flying in at his own expense the best doctor to heal them or, if that failed, a notable for the last rites.

I came to love him as the recruit loves the shrewd, tough, and vulgar commanding officer who swaggers and profanes too much in order to hide fears more threatening than the private's. He had the passion for fame that is the force of all great ambitions, but he suffered violent dissent in the ranks of his own personality. He is, in death as in life, damned to everlasting scrutiny.

If character is destiny, choice is history. Long after the last witness to those days is dead and buried, the consequences of Lyndon Johnson's decisions will be studied, sifted, and weighed for the manner in which they turned, to large or trivial directions, the tributaries of the American experience.

I have for a long time been reluctant to speak about the Johnson years for fear of unwittingly revising a history I did not understand even as I lived it. Perhaps Freud was right when he said that we all experience our presence naively. I certainly experienced it frenetically, possessed of far more energy than wisdom. Even now I am tentative about how all the pieces fit together. Only as I listen to others who shared the time and scholars who are examining it do I understand why I still believe and doubt.

On the plane back from Dallas that dark Friday afternoon, he was as he had always been—a man of infinite practicality unencumbered by theory. He once told me that every experience creates a new reality, and a good politician takes his mandate from opportunity. He reveled in the vocation of politics, and—in the Senate especially—his mastery of it, yielding here, standing firm there, then delaying again before acting to resolve the conflicting forces and interests. Huey Long of Louisiana used to talk about the difference between a scrooch owl and a hoot owl. "A hoot owl," said Huey, "bangs into the roost and knocks the hen clean off and catches her, but a scrooch owl slips into the roost, scrooches up to the hen and talks softly to her, and the hen just falls in love, and the next thing you know there ain't no hen." Lyndon Johnson was both a scrooch owl and a hoot owl.

The ancient Greeks employed two words for time. One was *chronos,* from which comes our word *chronology.* It meant time as a measurable quantity, the regular march of seconds into minutes and hours. If you ask me for the time, I'll give you *chronos.* The second word was *kyros,* a critical and decisive point that, taken boldly, becomes fateful. Euripides described this kind of time as the moment when "he who sees the helm of fate, forces fortune." The scribes in the New Testament used this term to suggest the fullness of time. Lyndon Johnson on that plane that afternoon believed he had come to power in just such a time.

Grasping though he had been in life, however, no amount of wily exertion would have brought him the office now delivered by a cruel and capricious fate. Only days before, he had said to friends that his future was behind him. Now suddenly he sought to consummate it in a swift and decisive series of events that would give his country and the world their first impression of him. With a materially decisive sense of the fateful, acting from the accumulated experiences of a lifetime in public office, and with antennae that swept the political landscape of Washington like the strong beam of a searchlight, he reckoned in those first few days to complete the agenda in waiting—and to shape his own. "This is the time to act," he said as he dressed that first fall day in office. Sure enough, by nightfall that same day he had instructed his chief economic adviser to proceed full steam ahead on planning the antipoverty program. Within days he met with the leaders of every major civil rights organization in the country, called in the powers in Congress, talked to old friends and new advisers. On the map of his mind there was already appearing in bold relief the routes he would ask the country to follow. No detour yet marked the exit of Vietnam. That would come later.

This was, thought LBJ, the fullness of time economically. Our resources were growing at the rate of 5 percent a year, and his economic advisers assured him (in the words of Walter Heller) that "in our time, the engine of our economy would be the mightiest engine of human progress the world has ever seen." Just by shifting a small portion of the additional resources created by growth, it was thought, we could abolish poverty without raising taxes. The Council of Economic Advisers had been created only in 1946. The measurement of our GNP as the chief indicator of economic performance and growth was established as an official government task only twenty years before LBJ became president. Already economists had been enshrined as the great reckoners of cost: their science was dubbed dismal because the first and foremost principle concerned itself with scarcity. One of the greatest principles of economics, said the economist Kenneth Boulding, had been enunciated by the duchess in *Alice in Wonderland,* "The more there is of yours, the less there is of mine," but now the economists were changing their tune and inviting all of us to sing with them, "More for everybody and more for me, too." Lyndon Johnson came to believe that we could all join in that delightful, positive-sum game of getting richer together. This, said one observer, was a time "when the number of chickens comfortably exceeded the number of pots."

He thought this was the fullness of time politically as well. Twenty-five years ago scholars and political observers had been debating the deadlock of democracy, the impasse of a system choked on huge, indigestible issues. Now a country shocked by the murder of John F. Kennedy yearned for proof the system could work again. It had in Lyndon Johnson a virtuoso of Washington politics. For him happiness was something for everybody. The British journalist Godfrey Hodgson would write that Johnson's ambition to build a great society was not the vulgar megalomania it was pictured to be. "Here instead," said Hodgson, "was one of those rare moments when a government had real freedom to compose a national agenda, with some assurance that it would be able to do most of the things it chose to do, because they were economically and politically affordable."

This was also for Lyndon Johnson the fullness of time personally. As a young congressman from the hill country of Texas, he had been what Theodore White calls a "country liberal." He supported rural electrification, social security, soil conservation, farm price supports, and federal aid to build power. Ambition turned him to the right. Running for the Senate, he probed for the core of a statewide constituency more conservative than those central Texas voters who first sent him to the House to do Franklin Roosevelt's bidding. To win the support of powerful business interests, he supported the Taft-Hartley Act to curb labor. In his successful race for the Senate in 1948, he denounced as socialized medicine what sixteen years later as president he would hail as salvation for the elderly. In that same race he condemned the civil rights portion of Harry Truman's Fair Deal as "a farce and a sham"—an effort, he said, to set up a police state in the guise of history.

But while he was a man of his time and place, he felt the bitter paradox of both. I was a young man on his staff in 1960 when he gave me a vivid account of that southern schizophrenia he understood and feared. We were in Tennessee. During the motorcade he spotted some ugly racial epithets scrawled on signs held by a few plain—he called them homely—white women on the edge of a crowd on a street corner. Late that night in the hotel, when the local dignitaries had finished the last bottle of bourbon and branch water and departed, he started talking about those signs, and long past midnight, with an audience of one, he was still going on about how poor whites and poor blacks had been kept apart so they could be separately fleeced.

> I'll tell you what's at the bottom of it. If you can convince the lowest white man he's better than the best colored man, he won't notice you're picking his pocket. Hell, give him somebody to look down on, and he'll empty his pockets for you. But even the best politician, even those on the little man's side, drew the line at color. They might read Shakespeare and quote Shelley, but out there in the crowds they shouted, "Nigger, nigger, nigger!"

He said if he could talk to just one man who had passed through the Senate before him, it wouldn't be Daniel Webster or Henry Clay or any of the other great figures other men might summon. The senator with whom he would have conversed was "Pitchfork Ben" Tillman—Benjamin Ryan Tillman of South Carolina. "Here," said LBJ, "was a fella who stood up for the farmers and sent the bankers and the lawyers packing. Here was a fella who took on the railroads, started colleges, and invited women to get a first-class education and persuaded the legislature to jack up money for schools. And yet," said Lyndon Johnson that night, "here was a fella who wanted to repeal the Fifteenth Amendment, who took the vote away from the colored folks, who got so passionate about these things that he almost got kicked out of the United States Senate." Except for the poison of race, "he might have been president of the United States. I'd like to sit with him and ask how it was to throw it away for the sake of hating." Some years later when his old friend Richard Russell of Georgia had left the White House after a visit, the president said, "God damn it. Jim Crow put a collar on more smart men as sure as if they were sentenced to a chain gang in Georgia. If Dick Russell hadn't had to wear Jim Crow's collar, Dick Russell would be sitting here now instead of me."

So for Lyndon Johnson, who once could look right through blacks, the presidency offered a reprieve from the past. At a press conference in the East Room a reporter unexpectedly asked the president how he could explain his sudden passion for civil rights when he had never had much enthusiasm for the cause. The question hung in the air. I could see those huge nostrils flare as the president stared directly at the reporter. I could almost hear the cue cards flipping through his mind and his silent cursing of a press secretary who had not anticipated this one. But then he relaxed, and from an instinct no assistant could brief—one seasoned in the double life from which he was now delivered and hoped to deliver others—he said in effect: "Most of us don't have a second chance to correct the mistakes of our youth. I do and I am." That evening sitting in the White House, discussing the question with friends and staff, he looked around the room, gestured broadly about the mansion where he was living, and said, "Eisenhower used to tell me that this place was a prison. I never felt freer."

Roy Wilkins of the NAACP came to the White House soon after the president, in a historic speech long to be remembered, declared to the Congress and the nation, "We shall overcome." Wilkins said he wept as the president moved toward the climactic moment when he put the whole armor of the White House behind the conscience of the nation. Now, waiting for the president to finish a phone call, Wilkins recalled how, as Senate majority leader, LBJ had perfected "the three-two trot of racial progress: three steps forward and two steps back." But "ever since he got in there," Wilkins said, pointing toward the Oval Office, "it's been rock around the clock," and so it had. For weeks in 1964 the president carried in his pocket the summary of a Census Bureau report showing that the lifetime earnings of an average black college graduate were actually lower than that of a white man with an eighth-grade education. When the *New York Times* in November 1964 reported racial segregation actually to be increasing instead of disappearing, he took his felt tip pen, scribbled across the article "Shame, shame, shame," and sent it to Everett Dirksen, the Republican leader in the Senate.

I have a hard time explaining to our two sons and daughter that when they were little children America was still deeply segregated. The White House press corps, housed in Austin when the president was on vacation in Texas, would often go to the faculty club at the University of Texas, which was still off-limits to blacks in 1964. I remember the night it changed. There was a New Year's party for one of the president's favorite assistants, Horace Busby. About halfway into the evening, there was a stir and everyone looked up. The president of the United States was entering with one of his secretaries on his arm—a beautiful black woman. A professor of law at the University of Texas, Ernest Goldstein, had come to the club that evening out of friendship for Busby, although he resented and had opposed the club's segregationist policies. Now, joyously but incredulously, he slipped up to me and asked, "Does the president know what he's doing?" "He knows," I said, but I wasn't sure. The next day Goldstein called the club to announce he intended to bring some black associates to a meeting there. "No problem at all," said the woman on the phone. "Are we really integrated?" Goldstein asked. "Yes, sir," she answered, "the president of the United States integrated us last night."

In those days our faith was in integration. The separatist cries would come later, as white flight and the black power movement ended the illusion that an atmosphere of genuine acceptance and respect across color lines would overcome in our time the pernicious effects of racism, so deeply embedded in American life. But Lyndon Johnson championed that faith. He genuinely believed that money spent on integrated education would produce greater equality in scholastic achievement and greater equality in society as well. He thought the opposite of integration was not just segregation but disintegration—a nation unraveling.

America *was* a segregated country when LBJ came to power. It *wasn't* when he left. But I am certain he would be appalled to discover today how many American blacks are still caught in the undertow of discrimination: the circle of segregated slum housing leading to inferior schooling, underemployment, broken homes, and low incomes, which lead inevitably back to segregated slums. He knew instinctively, I think, the peril of this disastrous converging of class and color. Whatever his motives—whether from a moral imagination now free from expediency or from expediency now free to seize a higher ground—he swore in those very first hours in office that he would move to combat on a broad front.

But he also knew that not an inch would be won cheaply. The Civil Rights Act of 1964 is to many of us a watershed in American history and one of the most exhilarating triumphs of the Johnson years. With it, blacks gained access to public accomodations across the country. When he signed the act he was euphoric, but late that very night I found him in a melancholy mood as he lay in bed reading the bulldog edition of the *Washington Post* with headlines celebrating the day. I asked him what was troubling him. "I think we just delivered the South to the Republican party for a long time to come," he said.

Throughout that heady year, even as his own popularity soared, the president saw the gathering storm of a backlash. George Wallace took 34 percent of the presidential vote in liberal Wisconsin, 30 percent in Indiana, and 43 percent in Maryland. Watching the newscasts one night, the president said, "George Wallace makes these working folks think whatever is happening to them is all the Negro's fault. He runs around throwing gasoline on coals that ought to be dying out; he'd burn down the whole goddam house just to save his separate drinking water." Once Whitney Young of the National Urban League came to visit, and the president sent me searching for a copy of Wallace's defiant proclamation for the preservation of segregation. Over and over he read it aloud, "Segregation now, segregation tomorrow, segregation forever!" Then he handed it to Whitney Young and said, "Remember that when you think we are about to cross the Jordan."

LBJ wanted to cross the Jordan, all right, and take everybody else with him. In those days he longed to integrate us all. He called in business, labor, the clergy; he even went skinny-dipping in the White House pool with Billy Graham before dressing in black tie for dinner with Cardinal Spellman. He called in ethnic groups, trade associations, schoolchildren, and graduate students. Liz Carpenter has reminded us of the time the president appointed fifty-three women to office with a single announcement. Someone sent him a copy of Thomas Jefferson's statement that "the appointment of a woman to office is an innovation for which the public is not prepared, nor am I." "Well," said LBJ, "I'm damn sure ready!" And he handed the quote to an aide with orders to find a qualified woman to name as an ambassador before the week was over. Which was done.

Critics attacked his notion of consensus, but the president kept insisting to some of us that in politics you cast your stakes wide and haul up a big tent with room for everybody who wants in. The only time I can remember any kind of discussion with him about his political philosophy, he said he was "a little bit left, a little bit right, and a lot of center." Peter Drucker wrote at the time that President Johnson's Great Society "represents a first response to some of the new issues, both at home and abroad. But it approaches those largely within the old alignments. It appeals primarily to the old values and it employs mostly the traditional rhetoric. The voice is Jacob's but the hands are the hands of Esau."

I am one of those who think it worked. I agree with scholars such as Jonathan Schwartz who believe those policies in 1964 and 1965 had a positive impact. Largely because of the baby boom and the huge increase in the number of women wanting jobs, 55 million Americans poured into the workforce from 1965 to 1980. As Schwartz points out, no other major Western nation experienced soaring birthrates spanning the two decades following World War II, which caused our workforce to increase by an extraordinary 40 percent. Unemployment could not help but rise, and it did: by 2.5 percent between 1965 and 1980. Yet the number of jobs almost doubled, in no small part the result of economic and social policies begun in the Johnson years and intended mostly to propel the growth of the private economy. It seems to me we can fairly ask what might have happened if the crowded baby boom generation had arrived in the workforce without those jobs.

On poverty LBJ was often of two minds simultaneously. One was traditional; the other flirted with the radical. Poverty could be ended, he believed, if the economy grew and the poor were better managed and trained for better jobs. Help them to a better doctor, move them into a better house. He remembered those Mexican children who couldn't read or write, and he told me a dozen times at least that he would have missed it all if he hadn't stayed in school. "I didn't learn a whole lot in classes in college, but I made a lot of contacts and sure learned how to get ahead," he said. That was education to LBJ: get up and get out. So with school, training, and equal opportunity poor people would make the system work for them. "Give them skills and rewards and they will become tax-payers instead of tax eaters," he said. When he signed into law the antipoverty program he said, "You tell Sargent Shriver no doles, we don't want any doles."

But as Franklin Roosevelt did, he thought the government should be adventuresome. He was willing to experiment. He thought there would be time to find out what worked and what didn't. He turned around the direction of one meeting on the budget by saying, "You know, you can't take a tank from the blueprint to the battlefield; you test it over and over. That's true of social programs as well. You can't take a poor kid and turn him around just by getting Congress to pass a bill and the president to sign it and one of those agencies in Washington to run it. You have to experiment and keep at it until you find what it takes." So if he shared the liberal faith that by enlarging the size of the economic pie of total income everyone would gain, he instinctively sensed it wasn't enough. As he said once, "Sometimes when that tide raises all those boats, some of those boats got leaks in the bottom." And he said if income grew without any change in relative shares, there would be no increase in equality. He certainly wasn't a flat-equality man, but he believed equality was the moving horizon that America had been chasing for all of its history.

Moreover, LBJ believed, income was not the only measure of well-being. Here he was getting a little daring. What about such goods of the public household as schools and police protection? Quality schools, quality protection: those were assets the poor would never be able to afford for want of personal income. "We wouldn't leave poor people undefended just because they couldn't buy a piece of the Air Force or the Navy," he told me. Why leave them uneducated and unhoused for the same reason? Status, self-respect, opportunities for upward mobility and political power— could these be left only to those who could afford them? "Not on your life," he said. I'm pretty sure LBJ never read John Stuart Mill, but in his bones, planted there from the experience of childhood and youth, he believed that in the absence of its natural defenders the interests of the excluded are always in danger of being over-looked.

So with no popular mandate except the conviction that what the best and wisest parents want for their child, the community should want for all its children, he okayed an antipoverty program that would try an end run around deeply ingrained institutional obstacles to social justice. It was a token, a start, but in the words of one observer, it also represented "a real social invention which may have large consequences for the future and the whole idea that the poor should organize themselves." In his more expansive moments LBJ talked of going all the way—of rebuilding the cities, restoring the countryside, redeeming public education. "It isn't enough just to round out the New Deal," he said one day to a congressman. "There has to be a better deal." He talked of the "Great Society," but the slogan was no more precise than others in currency in those days: Nelson Rockefeller's "Just Society," Ronald Reagan's "Creative Society," Barry Goldwater's "Free So-ciety." Sometimes LBJ choked on the term. It just didn't fit his way of talking. In the simplest terms, he was trying to raise our sights beyond sheer size and the grandeur of wealth: a full stomach, yes, but a fuller life, too.

One day he asked for a genealogy of the phrase. We searched, and there in the family tree of its forebears was this passage from Adam Smith's *The Wealth of Nations:*

According to the system of natural liberty, the sovereign has only three duties to attend to. Three duties of great importance indeed, but plain and intelligible to common understandings: First, the duty of protecting the society from the violence and invasion of other independent societies. Secondly, the duty of protecting as far as possible, every member of the society from the injustice or oppression of every other member of it, or the duty of establishing an exact administration of justice; and thirdly, the duty of erecting and maintaining certain public works and certain public institutions which can never be for the interest of any individual or small number of individuals to erect and maintain because the profit could never repay the expense to any individual or small number of individuals, though it may frequently do much more than repay it to a great society.

"That's it," LBJ said. "That's it. I'm an Adam Smith man."

He could talk privately as he talked publicly. "Let's conquer the vastness of space, create schools and jobs for everyone. Let's care for the elderly, let's build schools and libraries, let's increase the affluence of the middle class. Let's improve the productivity of business, let's do more for civil rights in one Congress than in the last one hundred years combined, and let's get started in all of these by summer"—with no increase in spending, at least not yet. "Ease into first gear and later on we'll shove the accelerator to the floor."

He really did believe he might have it all ways. "We can continue the Great Society while we fight in Vietnam," he told the country. Friend or foe, scholar or laity, champion or critic, if you would understand him, you must see that both, to him, were the unfinished business of his generation. With his domestic programs he would consummate a long tradition of social and economic reform. They were linked in his mind to Theodore Roosevelt's crusades against monopolies, FDR's regulatory intervention in the economy, Harry Truman's assumption of responsibility for full employment, and John Kennedy's emerging commitment to the abolition of poverty. Hans Morganthau was a critic of the president's foreign policy, but of LBJ's Great Society vision in 1965 he said, "It is oriented toward an intelligible and generally accepted

set of values. It seeks the enhancement and ultimate consumma-
tion of the individual's dignity and self-sufficiency."

So, to the president, was Vietnam a piece of America's Cold
War tradition of opposing communism where not to do so might
affect adversely the nation's interests. If he could do it without
troops, as Truman did in Greece, he would; if he could do it with
only the implied threat of force, as Kennedy had done in the
Cuban missile crisis, he would. But, he said, if it took force, as Truman had to use force in Korea, he would do that, too. What was
new was the president's decision to put those intentions into effect
simultaneously. It proved an improvident and costly combination.
The result in Vietnam was a loss out of proportion to the ends
sought. The increasing cruelty and futility of it sapped his morale
and vigor, robbed him of the tolerance and tranquility he always
had difficulty negotiating from the warring factions of his own
nature. The unconscious impulses that sometimes stormed his ego
and which not even Lady Bird could quiet whipped him into fits
of depression and delusion.

At home, his cherished consensus eroded into strenuous and violent political conflict. This might well have happened if there
had been no Vietnam War. We had the first hint of it in the racial
riots in Rochester, New York, in 1964, a preview of things to
come. But there was also no way the more ambitious policies
could have failed to eventually provoke the ire of many of those
interests on which consensus relied. This, too, was signaled early.

Sometime in the spring of 1965 I read and sent to the president
an essay by Herbert Marcuse applauding LBJ's objectives but
doubting the government's ability to stay the course. "Rebuilding
the cities, restoring the countryside, redeeming the poor, and re-
forming education," said Marcuse, "could produce nondestructive
full employement. This requires nothing more, nothing less than

the actual reconstruction outlined in the president's program. But the very program requires the transformation of power structures standing in the way of its fulfillment."

I underlined the part of the article that dealt with highway beautification, so dear to Lady Bird. It was a modest program, but Marcuse had seized upon it as a shining example of how he thought the president's ambitions irreconcilable with capitalist interests. The rigidly enforced elimination of all billboards, neon signs, and other commercial blights on nature meant the abrogation of some of the most powerful lobbies in the country. Marcuse felt the president wouldn't go this far.

"Who is this fellow Marcuse?" the president demanded on the phone.

I explained that he was a philosopher who had fled Germany when Hitler came to power, that he was teaching at Brandeis University, where some of his students thrilled to his ideas about revolution and radical politics, and that his book *One Dimensional Man* was being widely read on other campuses, too.

"What are you doing reading him?" the president asked.

"Well, I'm trying to keep up," I answered. "I even read Barry Goldwater's *Conscience of a Conservative* last year and sent it over to you, remember?"

"Well," he said, "don't send this fella's book, but call him and tell him Lady Bird's the revolutionary on this bill. Not me!"

Actually, both the president and Mrs. Johnson initially lobbied hard for the Highway Beautification Act, but in the end we compromised almost to the point of capitulation. The legislation passed, but it since has been so weakened by loopholes and tax enforcement that recently the *Wall Street Journal* said, "It protects the billboards more than it causes their removal."

Then there was the call I got from Richard Daley (as so many others did, too). Almost before I could say hello he asked, "What in hell are you people doing? Does the president know he's putting money in the hands of subversives?" Richard Daley's definition of subversion was the intervention of anyone outside his political machine. Suddenly the president was pouring money— "M-O-N-E-Y," Daley spelled it on the phone to me—"to people that aren't part of our organization." Didn't the president know they'd use that money to bring him down?

I don't think I'll ever know whether LBJ knew in advance that the community action program was going to generate so much political controversy. He did say to Sargent Shriver and others that we couldn't fight poverty from some of the traditional agencies of government, especially the older ones; he knew from twenty-five years in Washington that bureaucracies are inert. He said, "You'll have to run some guerrilla raids" around the traditional agencies, outflanking them and getting that help directly to the poor. This inevitably meant challenging the political status quo, and in Chicago, Richard Daley was Mayor Status Quo. When I told the president about Daley's call, he immediately phoned the mayor with a message the contents of which were never divulged to me because I had been by then disinvited from the scene. I found out only recently, from Wilbur Cohen, that the community action director eventually hired for Chicago was one of Richard Daley's own men. The operative saying goes, "He might be a subversive, but he's our subversive."

Again, such conflicts would have been serious enough without the Vietnam War, but an unpopular war caused defection by people who might otherwise have supported the changes envisioned by the new policies. I barely noticed at the time that in 1964 student rebels in Berkeley were uttering their first obscenities in the cause of free speech. Thoreau had urged nineteenth-century dissidents to "let your lives be a counter friction to stop the machine." Now Mario Savio was calling for students to put their bodies on the machine and stop it.

When the Berkeley uprising was followed by the escalation of the war in Vietnam and the draft began, the call to the young to stop the machine took on an urgent and personal meaning. Pickets showed up across from the White House wearing huge IBM cards that read, "I am a student. Do not fold, spindle, or mutilate." Burners of draft cards and advocates of Viet Cong victory were joined by young people who felt, for many other reasons, deeply alienated from American society.

Opponents of the war and critics of the Great Society were soon finding one another's company against a government that was their common foe. Lyndon Johnson belonged to the generation that saluted when the commander in chief said, "Do your duty." Now he began to confuse patriotism with blind loyalty. Dissent began as the mischief of "nervous Nellies" and then became the work of traitors. The more he sought to drive them to the fringe of the public square, the more the square blazed with the fires of his own effigies. By 1967, neither the president nor the country talked anymore of a grand vision.

I had left early that year, my morale hemorrhaging from self-inflicted wounds and from those unintended blows two proud and sensitive people suffer in the turbulent close quarters of a relationship so personal it cannot be mediated and so painful it cannot be continued. When I told him I was leaving he had me come to the ranch and for several hours the two of us drove around the pastures as he talked almost without interruption. Once he said, "If I had to do it over again, I'd come to the White House as a presidential assistant, not as president."

"Why?" I asked.

"Because you can quit and I can't."

He had talked at times to Mrs. Johnson and others of not wanting to run again, but then he would talk of what remained to be
done once he brought the boys home from Vietnam. Now, out
there on the rim of a hill overlooking the pasture, he leaned
against the steering wheel and said, "We'll just be getting to the
end of the runway with that first term and we'll be taking off on
the second. You ought to be around for the takeoff." But he didn't
sound as if he himself relished the trip or believed that it would really happen. He seemed to know the fullness of time had come
and passed.

What worked? Well, in 1967, 75 percent of all Americans over
sixty-five had no medical insurance and a third of the elderly lived
in poverty. More than 90 percent of all black adults in the South
were not registered to vote, and across the nation there were only
about two hundred elected officials who were black. There was
no Head Start for kids. Today, Medicare, food stamps, and more
generous Social Security benefits have helped reduce the poverty
rate for the elderly by half, and they are no poorer than Americans
as a whole. Nearly six thousand blacks hold elected office, including the office once held by Richard Daley. A majority of small
children attend preschool programs. The bedrock of the Great
Society—Medicare, Medicaid, federal aid to education, the right
of blacks to citizenship—are permanent features of the American
system, so much so that in the first debate between Ronald Reagan and Walter Mondale, Reagan presented himself as the man
who saved your safety net.

What went wrong? Some things that went wrong were unjustly blamed on the Great Society. As my former colleague Ben
Wattenberg has pointed out, there was no "soft-on-crime act" of
1966. There was no "permissive-curriculum act" of 1967. There
was no "get-vindictive-with-business act" of 1968. But plenty of
things went wrong. Progress fell victim to pork-barrel politics.

The idea of giving the poor resources for leadership never got the support it deserved. Employment training projects suffered from high dropout rates, there were often no jobs when the training ended, and the programs' cost exceeded the estimate.

We had jumped too fast, spread out too thinly over too vast a terrain, and then went to war on a distant front against an enemy that would not bargain, compromise, or reason but wanted only to win. For once in his career, Lyndon Johnson sat down at the table, divided up the chips, cut the cards—and no one showed up to deal.

A slogan is a dangerous thing. Those who create it can lose control of its meaning. Others read into it what was not there. Friends put their own spin on it. It can mean everything or nothing. But slogans aside, at the root of the Great Society was only an idea— and not a new one. It was the idea that free men and women can work with their government to make things better. Lyndon Johnson's generation had been traumatized by the Great Crash, by the sight of lean and hungry men wandering the countryside in search of food and work, by the collapse of the economic system they had trusted. His generation came to maturity at a time when state governments were failing or verged on bankruptcy. Only the national government could move to help. And many of the local governments were as morally bankrupt in matters of race as they were financially woeful, masquerading in the highfalutin rhetoric of states' rights. They held themselves up as the arbitrary judges of their own conduct no matter how unjust or dangerous to the social fabric.

Furthermore, by the time Lyndon Johnson reached the White House, the United States was in the throes of one of the most perplexing and painful transitions in its history. We were becoming a national society with an intricately intertwined economy, a metropolitan society with many people living in a small number of densely populated areas, a pluralistic society with huge organizations with multitudes of activities that must mesh to make the system work.

Government did not grow bigger and become more centralized on a whim or a caprice. Big government was the response to two world wars, the Cold War, the Great Depression, urbanization, an unjust social system, and market forces that did not stay around to help losers. Big government is symptomatic of the fact that modern society depends on a far-reaching and complex organizational network that extends across the nation and the world. The health and welfare of each member of this society is dependent on the health and welfare of the whole enterprise.

In the old mythology of Hollywood westerns, the rugged individual rides alone toward the sunset without the thought of a Holiday Inn at the next exit ramp or whether the food has been inspected. But there is no escape for us today to some simpler place like the good old days. Ronald Reagan has not presided over a diminishing of government. Rather, he has shifted resources from social services to the defense establishment. The result is not a reduction in federal spending but a doubling of the national debt in five years with a higher percentage of the gross national product going to government than when he entered office. The problem of big government is real. Finding ways to make this complex system work, of making it responsive and responsible with due regard for the integrity of the individual and the well-being of the country, was the challenge we set out to wrestle. It will continue far into the future.

"The Great Society," said Lyndon Johnson, "is a challenge constantly renewed." Back in 1964, Syracuse University convened a scholarly seminar on the Great Society, and President Johnson proposed that the scholars consider five questions. The scholars turned them into two. Just what is the Great Society, and what should become its content? How can we best measure desired and actual change in any society? The first has to do with the most complex and controversial aspects of human values, national purposes, and political leadership. The second goes to the heart of our ability to understand the complexity of social reality. If Lyndon Johnson were around today, he would badger, poke, parry, and above all listen—eager to hear everybody's answers to those questions.

—1986

GOOD FRIEND

Seminarian, preacher, politician, educator, federal official, ambassador, businessman, citizen: this is how the world remembers William Herbert Crook. Here's the Bill I remember. Consider yourself among the fortunate of the world if you have just one friend like him:

- Who tells you the truth when the world is seducing you with flattery, or, when it lets fly its slings and arrows, reassures you these things, too, shall pass

- Who comes two thousand miles to arrive unexpectedly as your daughter is undergoing brain surgery and endures with you the long, slow hours until the surgeon appears and says, "It's over. She's okay."

- Who calls out of the blue on a winter morning with a simple declaration: "Just wanted you to know I'm thinking about you, buddy"

- Who, seeing the shadow on your heart, interrupts a long silence on the veranda, as the light descends from a mantle of white stone above the gorge at the edge of an old Spanish town, to summon from his beloved Browning an affirmation: "Earth changes, but thy soul and thy God are sure"

How do you get such a friend? Mere coincidence? Well, yes, if coincidence is God's way of remaining anonymous. Bill asked me this question the last time we were together, a few weeks before his death. "How do you explain our friendship?" he asked.

I couldn't. "I remember the facts," I said. "But the magic—I can't explain the magic."

He was older, which to his chagrin I never let him forget, but there were parallels and patterns. We married the same year, 1954, to equally great-hearted women who were themselves kindred spirits. And we admitted to one another that marriage had been the rock of our lives and the anchor of our long four-square friendship. At breakfast this morning Judith was reviewing the extraordinary fight that Bill and Eleanor had made over the past twelve years since they discovered his health to be in jeopardy: how formidable and ingenious the threat and how sustained and collaborative a resistance they mounted together. Without Eleanor's strength and her strategy Bill would not have lived to see his seven grandchildren born. To Judith and me it was clear that from his relationship with Eleanor sprang the deepest joy of his accomplished life.

He was a Baptist, and so was I. He graduated from Southwestern Seminary, and so did I. He did postgraduate work at the University of Edinburgh in Scotland, and I followed. He even moved to east Texas, an hour from where I grew up. Still, we hadn't met when I went to Washington in January 1960 to work for Senator Lyndon B. Johnson. Reading the paper in my office one morning, I noticed an Associated Press story from Nacogdoches, Texas, with a headline that announced "Baptist Pastor Resigns Pulpit to Run for Congress." I showed it to Senator Johnson, who said, with a grin, "Must be a Baptist twist—if you can't join 'em, beat 'em." Bill's opponent in the primary was an entrenched, corrupt incumbent (who finally wound up in prison), and I was struck that so promising a young preacher would risk so much to take him on. First Church, Nacogdoches, was a plum in those days, the closest we came in east Texas to a Baptist diocese, and I was impressed that Bill would give it up to redefine his calling beyond the pulpit into the precinct of politics. So I wrote a short note of encouragement and sent a small check to his campaign. I thought it was for $50, but Bill insisted, down to our last meeting a few weeks ago, that it was only $15. The way he handled a collection plate, no wonder he couldn't stay a Baptist.

He lost the primary. East Texans didn't know what to make of an honest Crook; after Nixon made his famous declaration, "I am not a crook," Bill called me and said, "I can't tell you how relieved I am he's resigned from the family." He lost, but he and Eleanor had cut such a swath of vigor and character through the piney-wood crudities of yellow dog politics that I was eager to get acquainted. So one day I called Bill and we arranged to get together. We met in my room at Austin's Driskill Hotel, talked until midnight, moved to the all-night P.K. Grill on West Seventh Street, and when we finally paused to catch our breath, the sun was rising and the waitress was asking how we would like our eggs for breakfast. From then on the conversation never ended. Circumstances and duties kept interrupting it, but anything could jump-start it again—a letter, a clipping in the mail, a telephone call, a story in the evening news. We could go from the sublime to the ridiculous in less time than it takes a period to end a sentence: from talking about whether a father can ever really know a daughter's hurt or a son's pride to whether Paul the Apostle was a misogynist, whether his father-in-law would ever forgive him for becoming an Episcopalian, and how many Sundays of sermons the fundamentalists in Texas could make of it if the two of us were arrested for smuggling a handful of Cuban cigars through customs on our way home from Europe.

The last time we met I asked him if he had any regrets. "Oh," he said, "I would like to have been better at public service." But then, echoing his old mentor Rabbi Ben Ezra, he said, "But what I aspired to be and am not, comforts me." There was a pause, and then he said, "I do have one big regret. I regret that when I was on the fast track back in Washington in the sixties I never realized the toll our life exacted from Eleanor and Bill junior and Noel and Mary Elizabeth. And I wish I could get those years over again." Well, that's my big regret, too, so we talked a long time— we two old men with our wounds from the follies of immature ambition.

But it was anything but morbid, our last time together—to the contrary. And his rendezvous with death included planning his funeral, down to instructions that no one was to soil the venture by tracking grief into the house. "That shall be tomorrow, not tonight," he told me, invoking his old friend Browning again. "Now I must bury sorrow out of sight." So he charged the household with purpose and recruited everyone in his path.

His dry wit could contain any contagion of pessimism or sentimentality. When he grew tired our last evening together, we went up on the elevator together to his bedroom. On the landing he looked at me and said, "Bill, my time will be over sooner than later, and I'm so glad you came." There was an awkward silence and a more awkward embrace, and then, as he started toward the bedroom, he looked down at the black Reeboks I had worn in my haste to get there, poked them with his silver-headed cane, and said, "Those are the ugliest shoes I've ever seen." And that was that. He governed the last moment. The doctor said he had a phenomenal capacity to hold such clarity with such concentration through the fog rising around him. The vigor of his mind was the engine of his lifelong curiosity.

I had a letter from him a few months ago. "Have you read 'The

Hound of Heaven' by Francis Thompson lately?" he asked. "It's one of the most powerful poems ever written and at present I'm reading it aloud once a day to improve my diction." Last night I browsed his library again, as I've done often through the years. All of Shakespeare's there, and Dickens and Churchill, Bingley's *Animal Biography*, Pepys' *Diary*, James Fenimore Cooper, Jules Verne, Carl Sandburg's *Lincoln*—even Rayback's biography of Millard Fillmore. But his preference was always Browning. Look through his collected works of Browning and you'll see those dog-eared pages, the underlined sentences, the little clippings with notations: all the signature of a continuing interrogation. He read and remembered, and even as he was still barely able to speak he was recollecting. His sister Eileen asked him the source of one passage recently, and he whispered, "I can't believe you're asking me that. It's Dickens. It's Dickens."

Visit the collection of the signed presidential books he gave the LBJ Library and you sense the fascination he had with American history and those who made it. His mother was born in India and his father in England, but together they produced an irrepressible American patriot who revered the men of learning who shaped our republic. When he finally secured a volume signed by our first president, he handed it to his friend and secretary, Joye Blankenship, and said, "Doesn't it give you a thrill knowing George Washington wanted this book, held it in his very hands, looked through its pages and wrote his name in it?" But it was not so much the thing itself he honored as the witness it offered to a life of passion tempered by reason. That's how he lived his own life, and you could see it in the trajectory of his own religious quest. Forced faith and uncritical obedience were anathema to Bill, and so were postures of piety. With Browning's Bishop Blougram he could honestly debate the choice between a life of doubt diversified by faith and one of faith diversified by doubt. And with the good old bishop he concluded, "You call for faith? I show you doubt to prove that faith exists. The more of doubt the stronger faith I say, if faith o'ercomes the doubt." The important thing, he said, is to work it through yourself: commitment, tempered by reason.

In his own time he had been a powerful public speaker. I was fortunate to hear what surely was one of his finest speeches. It was thirty-odd years ago, and he was national director of VISTA—Volunteers in Service to America, the domestic Peace Corps. Addressing a large assembly of volunteers just before they spread out across the country to their assignments, he took his text from James Thurber. Holding that audience in the palm of his hand, he drew them into a memorable meditation on the role of reason and conscience. This is how he ended, pure Bill Crook:

> In his short story "The Shore and the Sea" James Thurber tells of the lemmings, those strange little rodents of the Nordic countries who are accused of suicidal propensities that periodically they stampede by the thousands into the sea. The mass frenzy begins when, viewing the sunset on the ocean, a single excited lemming starts the exodus by crying "Fire!" and running toward the sea. "The world is coming to an end," he shouts. And as the hurrying hundreds turn to thousands the reasons for their headlong flight increase by leaps and bounds and hops and skips and jumps. Others begin to cry out that the devil has come in a red chariot. Still others that the world is on fire. The panic increases, the rumors multiply, and pandemonium prevails as the lemmings by the thousands leap into the sea and disappear beneath the waves, some crying, "We are saved," and some, "We are lost." An old, scholarly lemming watches the futile self-destruction of the mob, tears up all that he's written about the species, and starts all over again. The moral: All men should strive to learn before they die what they're running from, and to, and why.

Bill loved that story, and he lived that moral. He was not one to be stampeded. During a local controversy, he and Eleanor took a stand at odds with official opinion. They objected to an edict of conformity in the schools that they felt to be an infringement of their children's dignity. So they organized a protest and drove around town honking the horn of their car. No doubt it was the only demonstration in all of the sixties anywhere in America in which the rabble-rouser was driving a yellow Lamborghini. Tensions rose in town to such a pitch that some folks attempted to burn a cross on the Crooks' front lawn. This delighted Bill no end. "Terrific!" he said as he promptly began trying to decide where on the porch he could situate himself to best view the spectacle. But alas, when the moment arrived, the fire sputtered and died out of its own accord, and the perpetrators skulked off unrequited. Bill, too, felt cheated. "I've always wanted a cross burned on my front yard for doing the right thing," he said, "and when it finally happened, the damn thing wouldn't light."

Not even John Connally could intimidate him. The governor was coming to Washington to demand of the president that control of the regional War on Poverty be transferred from the Office of Economic Opportunity, headed by Bill Crook, to the governor's own office in Austin. Everyone assumed that LBJ would side with the governor, who had been his oldest and closest ally. But the president asked for some time with Bill before John Connally arrived, and put the question directly: "What's the right thing to do?" Bill looked him in the eye and said, "Mr. President, John Connally's a great governor and I know he's your good friend, but John Connally commits patronage, and this program should not be hostage to favor or partisanship." And with that Bill offered to leave so that the president and the governor could have time alone and the president would not be forced to choose between them face-to-face. But LBJ wouldn't have it; he insisted Bill stay, and when a few minutes later Governor Connally came striding in, he was greeted by the president, his arm draped around Bill Crook's shoulders, saying, "Well, John, Bill here thinks the poverty thing could blow up in your face, and out of respect for your promising future in national politics, he's reluctantly agreed to keep control so you won't have to take any blame." It's the only time in my life I saw John Connally speechless. But it wasn't the only time I saw Bill Crook swallow the canary.

He had, you see, the courage of his convictions, but he also had the more complex intuitive courage of character that moves one to do alone and unwitnessed what you would do if the whole world were watching. Back in 1985 Bill and Bill junior went to Ethiopia at the height of that country's civil war. They went at the request of the Bishop and under the auspices of the Presiding Bishop's Fund, which wanted Bill's advice on how the Anglican community could respond to the vast suffering of people destitute of hope. For a month, they visited the refugee camps, sinkholes of starvation and suffering and sickness, where people emaciated by diarrhea were being ravaged by cholera and hepatitis. Bishop Folts tells me that Bill's discernments were the architecture of the worldwide Anglican community's response to that suffering. But the trip also led to his own long illness, for while in those camps Bill was exposed to the stealth of some hostile microscopic aggressor that weakened and then ravaged him for years, and finally brought on his death. This old air force tail gunner from World War II was finally brought down on a mission of mercy. "Would you go again?" I asked him three Sundays ago. He looked at me and with that beautiful little smile said, "Of course. I'd go in an instant."

One last recollection: Judith and I were along with Bill and Eleanor when they traveled to Spain four years ago to secure for

Corpus Christi, Texas, the replicas of Christopher Columbus' caravels. Bill did the negotiating, Eleanor did the translating, and Judith and I did the cheerleading. He brought to the pursuit the poise, aplomb, and passion of a lifetime, and despite his failing health he seemed to relish every moment of the conquest: the protocol with Christopher Columbus' direct descendant, the Duke of Cologne; the tour of the old city of Toledo, led by the mayor; the quaint hotel in the old Jewish quarter of Seville; the soft light at dusk and the flamenco dancers at midnight; the visit to the estuary on the coast from which Columbus had sailed and the monastery where he had found refuge and knowledge for his belief that the seas could be navigated far beyond the horizon. But most of all, Bill relished the little town of Ronda, along a deep gorge in the southern mountains. We sat on the veranda watching the shadows fall on the far side of the divide, and I became aware of the intimations of mortality that gripped him. We talked about the miracle of birth and the mystery of death and all the surprises between, and how everything adds up, or doesn't. After a long silence he looked at those shadows and once again softly summoned Browning: "How good is man's life. The mere living, how fit to employ all the heart, and the soul, and the senses enjoy."

—1998

AGING

When the invitation to join AARP arrived in the mail I assumed it must have been wrongly addressed. Then one day I looked in the mirror and a senior citizen was looking back. Staring at me was someone old enough to be a member of the American Association of Retired People—born, as some peer once described our time, "before radar, credit cards, split atoms, laser beams and ballpoint pens; before pantyhose, dishwashers, clothes dryers, electric blankets, air conditioners, drip-dry clothes, and before man walked on the moon, before television, before penicillin, before polio shots, frozen foods, Xeroxes, plastic, contact lenses, and the Pill."

I never thought much about growing old. Most of us journalists are so obsessed with the here and now that we don't think about the future. Growing old happened only at the end of the trip, like arriving at the depot after a long train ride. One day we'd get off the train and be old. It wasn't a promising destination. My cousin in Texas sent me a column entitled "How to Tell You're Aging." It had been written with the bias of a time when it was socially acceptable to mock the old. "Aging," it said, "is when the gleam in your eyes is from the sun hitting your bifocals; when you feel like the night after, and you haven't been anywhere; when your little black book contains only names ending in M.D.; when you finally reach the top of the ladder and find it leaning against the wrong wall; when you decide to procrastinate but never get around to it; when your mind makes contracts your body can't meet; when you know all the answers but nobody asks you the questions; when you're 17 around the neck, 44 around the waist, and 96 around the golf course; when your favorite part of the newspaper is '25 Years Ago Today.' "

The author went on, but I didn't; that was enough for me. I didn't like the spin. "Old" happened to others. It didn't happen to me. But that fellow in the mirror—the one with the thinning hair graying all over; with little islands of brown floating in unwelcome places on his face, staring back at me through trifocals—who did I think that was? From one corner of my brain came a half-remembered epigram from long ago: "Age has crept upon thee unperceived." For his part Emerson had counseled: "It is time to be old. To take in sail." But I stared back hard at the stranger in the mirror and said, "To hell with you!" and decided not to shave right then.

But I knew that the very experience of time was making me an expert in aging, against my will. I decided to go for the good news about growing old, and I found it. For one thing, we're living longer. In the 4,500 years from the Bronze Age to the year 1900 life expectancy increased twenty-seven years, and in the short period from 1900 to now it increased by at least that much again. The change has been so dramatic, it is currently estimated that of all the human beings who have ever lived, half are currently alive. And with the baby boomers turning fifty years old, by 2010 there will be as many seniors as there are people under the age of twenty. Approximately three million of these elder boomers—according to the New England Centenarian Study—can expect to live to a hundred or more. So that's good news: death waits longer to come calling. When I was born—before penicillin—the median age at death was fifty-two. Now it's seventy-six.

Moreover, we're turning around the negative view of aging that once made old people the butt of so many jokes. In fact, *Successful Aging* is the title of the book based on a very important study sponsored by the MacArthur Foundation. Researchers had looked at more than one thousand highly functioning older people to determine the factors that predict successful physical and mental aging. Then the investigators did detailed studies of hundreds of pairs of Swedish twins to determine the genetic and lifestyle contributions to aging. Laboratory-based studies examined older people's response to stress. And the foundation sponsored nearly a dozen studies of brain aging in humans and animals.

Such studies have shattered the myths about aging that held older people hostage to caricature and stereotype. To summarize them is to affirm that we no longer believe that to be old is inevitably to be sick—we know now that we can reduce our risk of disease and disability. Nor do we still believe that "old dogs can't learn new tricks," for we know that old age can be a time for learning, that trained elders can even do better at memory games than untrained young people. We no longer believe that our course in old age is predetermined; we know from strong scientific evidence that successful aging is not for the most part inherited and that we are largely responsible for our own old age—we have the capacity to enhance our chance of maintaining high mental and physical ability as we grow older. Nor do we any longer believe that "the lights may be on, but the voltage is low," for we know that the basic human need for affectionate physical contact persists throughout life—and so does the capacity for giving it. We no longer believe that the elderly don't pull their own weight, that older people take more from society than they give back. We see too many who are still making a difference to someone, and very often to society, to count them useless. The most important thing we've learned about older people—about ourselves—is that attitude and activity matter.

What is attitude? The MacArthur study answers that question with an anecdote from Satchel Paige, the legendary black pitcher who was

> as famous for his fast answers as for his fastball. He began pitching at the age of seventeen and was for many years restricted to what was then called the Negro Baseball League. Born near the turn of the century, he was already a veteran at the pitcher's mound when the racial barrier was relaxed. However, the decades rolled by, and he continued to pitch. As he did so, Paige became purposefully vague about his age, a subject of increasing speculation among sportswriters. When one of them put the question bluntly, "How old *are* you?" Paige gave him a classic answer: "How old *would* you be if you didn't know how old you was?"

Or as Bernard Baruch said, "To me, old age is always ten years older than I am." Jesting aside, our attitude can shape the way that we age. Freud captured this in a letter to his daughter in 1908:

> You have, my poor child, seen death break into the family for the first time . . . and perhaps shuddered at the idea that for none of us can life be made any safer. This is something that all we old people know, which is why life for us has such a happy value. We refuse to allow the inevitable end to interfere with our happy activities.

In other words, affirming ourselves allows us to engage the world no matter our age. The MacArthur study showed clearly that "happy activities" are essential to successful aging. Once upon a time the main task of old age was defined as letting go: of jobs, friends, strenuous recreation, and life itself. And of course we can't deny that age brings loss: the death of friends and loved ones, the often ambivalent experience of retirement, the necessity of moving from familiar homes or neighborhoods. But we know from research and from experience that the very things that constitute well-being throughout the life course—close relationships with others, activities that we invest with meaning and purpose—are no less important in later life than in earlier life. Even as we adjust to changing circumstance we can adopt appropriate activities to compensate for the loss and affirm our lives anew.

Reduce all these studies to their essence and you have the three main components of successful aging, things so obvious today that they have become commonplace: avoid disease and disability, maintain mental and physical function, and continue to engage with life. Freud reduced those three components further into a very simple summary of what makes life viable at any age: love and work. The people who age successfully find new friends and new ways to be productive, maintain some regular exercise, and enjoy a measure of increased leisure. Life, for them, retains the capacity for wonder, surprise, and joy—especially the joy of the present experience.

Joseph Campbell pointed the way. The longtime teacher of comparative mythology at Sarah Lawrence College spent his life studying the great stories of the human race and how they help us explain to ourselves the universe and our relation to it. Among his numerous books was a classic many of us read in college, *The Hero with a Thousand Faces.* Of the hundreds of hours of programming I have helped to create over the past thirty years, none proved more popular or had more impact than *Joseph Campbell and the Power of Myth.* One reason was Campbell's own passion for life. He taught as great teachers teach, by example. It was not his manner to try to talk anyone into anything. Preachers make a mistake, he said, when they try to talk people into belief; better they reveal the radiance of their own discovery. Matthew Arnold once said that the highest form of criticism is "to know the best that is known and thought in the world, and by in its turn making this known, to create a current of true and fresh ideas." So it was with Campbell. It was impossible to listen to him without realizing in one's own consciousness a stirring of fresh life, the rising of one's own imagination.

In our last televised conversation he talked about the "guiding idea" of his work: to find "the commonality of themes in world myths, pointing to a constant requirement in the human psyche for a centering in terms of deep principles."

"You're talking about a search for the meaning of life," I said.

"No, no, no," he answered. "I'm talking about the *experience of being alive!*" He explained: "People say that what we're all seeking is a meaning for life. I don't think that's what we're really seeking. I think that what we're seeking is the experience of being alive, so that our life experiences on the purely physical plane will have resonances within our own innermost being and reality, so that we actually feel the rapture of being alive."

Remember the words of Tennyson's great poem "Ulysses":

> How dull it is to pause, to make an end,
> To rust unburnished, not to shine in use!
> As though to breathe were life!

I am reminded of two people who seem the very embodiment of those words. One is a woman named Flora Meyer Allen. She's ninety-seven and lives in California. She remembers being jolted awake by the San Francisco earthquake in 1906, of screaming her head off as the bottom of her crib fell down. She recently told the

Wall Street Journal that she remembers her brother holding her up and saying, "Look at San Francisco burn." It was, she said, like a beautiful sunset. For years Mrs. Allen ran her own garment factory stitching baby clothes and bridal gowns. When she closed her factory at age sixty, she took a job with an apparel firm. She's been a widow for half a century and lives alone in a suburban ranch house in Alameda, where she looks after her garden and antiques—and continues to joust with her three sisters, who are also in their nineties. Mrs. Allen says she didn't notice she was getting old until her eightieth birthday. That was the year she gave up spike heels.

Then there's Harvey Shapiro. He's nearly one hundred and has lived in Manhattan since 1905, when he came to America from Russia. He lived what he calls a sequestered life, eating carefully and drinking a little—just enough to be called a guy who likes a spot of whiskey. For sixty-five years he walked to his job as a commercial illustrator, and in the 1970s he retired to pursue his vocation, painting in oils and watercolors. Nowadays he eats a simple diet of fish and chicken, reads history books, and listens to Bach, whom he credits for contributing to his own longevity. Harvey's made only one concession to age. He's given up the violin, because, he says, "the fiddle is a young man's instrument."

I haven't met Harvey Shapiro or Flora Meyer Allen. I just read about them in a wonderful column in the *Wall Street Journal* by Marilyn Chase (January 14, 2000). Both are participating in a study of centenarians which finds that a surprising number of them play a musical instrument or speak at least a second language. Furthermore, the research also reveals that healthy hundred-year-olds seem to be remarkably low in neuroticism. They don't tend to brood or dwell on things, which of course is what we journalists do for a living.

So this is a good time to be aging, if you can afford it. Yet, one thing hasn't changed. No matter how well we age, the death rate remains the same: one per person. There's no way around it. Like most Americans, I'd rather not think about death, especially my own. Woody Allen famously said, "I'm not afraid of dying; I just don't want to be there when it happens." Same here. Thomas Lynch, the funeral director and poet, writes extensively about his work at the intersection of living and dying. In an interview for my series *On Our Own Terms* he says that although the two are inextricably linked, the distance we put between ourselves and our death turns it into an embarrassment or a spectacle:

> We go to see frightening movies. We love to see Arnold Schwarzenegger machine-gun a bazillion people all at once—we like death on that scale. And we like it on the scale where we can laugh about it—the Halloween thing. But the normal ground where people love and grieve, we are uncomfortable with. That huge middle ground most of us occupy, in which we form lifelong attachments that are broken by death—we don't like to talk about that.

We are reluctant to talk about death because it's an uncomfortable subject. It reminds us we're mortal; we're afraid of the unknown; we don't want to burden our families, so we defer the pain of preparing for the inevitable and we keep quiet about it. But it's no secret that we don't die well in America. This is a great place to be sick, because the odds are good that you'll get well. We have all this incredible medical technology that has given us unprecedented power to treat illness. But that very technology has also produced unintended consequences that have changed the experience of dying, consequences that include intense pain, financial devastation, and loss of self-determination. Before World War II— before antibiotics—usually death came quickly. Today, while many people who age are healthy and active, many are enduring prolonged deaths as a consequence of chronic, progressive disease, accompanied by great physical, emotional, existential, and spiritual suffering.

No one wants to die that way. We want a gentle closure, a good death. Recently I reviewed the results of a major study of Americans from various income and education levels, gender and age groups, religious and ethnic backgrounds. Whatever their background, people said they fear reaching the end of their lives hooked up to machines. They said they want a natural death in familiar surroundings with the people they love, and that they know what they want is not what our medical system and our culture provide. But because we're all so uncomfortable with the topic of death, we resist taking action to change the system and the culture; we're reluctant to take the steps necessary to prepare for the death we desire. Deep in the back of our minds we tell ourselves that our loved ones will make the right decisions for us when the time comes, that we don't have to tell them what we want.

But this situation is changing. After years of inattention, American society and American medicine are taking a fresh look at how we approach death and dying and how we care for people at the end of their lives. For our series *On Our Own Terms* we filmed all over the country to report on the growing movement to improve end-of-life care. Medicine and consumers alike are pioneering new ways to make our last passage more comfortable and free of pain. As one physician said to me, "What's happening today can only be compared to what we saw in the early days of the women's movement, when there was a groundswell of public support for the transformation of childbirth. Just as we made things better for the beginning of life, so are we going to make things better for the leaving of it."

Why is this happening now? For one thing, too many people

are dying deaths they deplore in places they despise. Ninety percent of the people in a Gallup poll said they want to die at home,
but in fact more than 80 percent of us will die in hospitals or nurs-
ing homes, and as many as 70 percent of us will die in pain.

My own mother died last April at the age of ninety-one. It was
the end of three hard years for her. I was in the room that day in
1996 when she visibly stopped aging and started dying. In an instant she was in the grip of another reality. Her forehead wrinkled,
her eyes closed, her jaw slackened, her hand tightened into a claw;
my mother disappeared at that moment and never came back to
us, although she did not die until three years later. I made a lot of
mistakes during that time. I didn't know about the breakthroughs
in pain management. I mistook the inscrutability of doctors for
authority, even wisdom. I didn't even know much about hospice
until it was almost too late. Simply put, I did not know how to
help my mother as she was dying. Unfortunately, there are no
charts at the end of a hospital bed to measure soul pain, and one
thing driving the movement to improve care at the end of life is
the desire for dignity and comfort.

Baby boomers are driving it, too. They're aware suddenly of
their own mortality. Some years ago baby boomers told George
Gallup that retirement was their greatest concern. They have
changed their tune; now their greatest concern is mortality, their
parents' and their own. The AIDS epidemic also brought death
and dying to the surface. It not only made the subject unavoid-
able, but also taught us something about care for the dying, because when the epidemic arrived with such sudden devastation,
neither the medical system nor the country was prepared for it.
Gay men and women had no alternative but to care for the victims themselves; no one knew anything else to do.

In my latest series on poets and poetry, *Fooling with Words,* the
poet Mark Doty tells about his own companion, who died a diffi-

cult death from AIDS. "This was a moment of profound hopelessness," he said. "Our lives had been scoured by the epidemic. Nothing had so inscribed and transformed my own experience as that whole constellation of events. I realized that all we had was our ability to take care of each other, to stand with each other. We had our dreams, we had the ways in which we negotiated privately with loss. It was imperative—or so it seemed to me—that we see ourselves as being part of a community of caretakers, dreamers, and mortal beings." What a difference it could make if all of us could realize that vision—could see ourselves as a community of caretakers, dreamers, and mortal beings who could do something then about a health care system that lets so many people die deaths they despise in places they deplore.

One other phenomenon has driven the movement to improve end-of-life care: the debate over physician-assisted suicide. I'm not proud of how my own craft of journalism has handled this debate. We've allowed Dr. Kevorkian to frame it in the most simplistic terms: are you for or against the right to commit suicide? That's not the question. The question is: how do we improve the quality of care whether physician-assisted suicide is possible or not? How do we address the fear that too much will be done to keep us alive or that not enough will be done? How do we see to it that we are not abandoned by our caregivers? How do we enable people to exercise more control over their dying—over how and where they die—while ensuring that they are not taken advantage of?

We need a new language to talk about these things. Families are often not prepared to make end-of-life decisions because they worry that talking about death hastens death. Just as sadly, doctors are not candid, either. In *On Our Own Terms* residents tell me they have come through seven years of medical school without a single course in end-of-life care. In one survey only 14 percent of the doctors said they had substantive conversations about the prognosis with their patients who are dying. Many doctors simply don't understand the hope for a good death, partly because they fear talking about it will cause their patients to quit fighting. So our model for death is the Dylan Thomas line "Rage, rage against the dying of the light," which we have turned into the motto "Go down with your guns blazing." We need a new vocabulary.

We also need to better comfort people who cannot be cured. I find it astonishing that we have made so much progress in pain management and yet so few dying people benefit from it. In one study (by Memorial Sloan-Kettering) patients reported experiencing thirteen kinds of intolerable symptoms, and half of those patients said they were being undertreated for the pain. Eighty-two percent of AIDS patients in another study said they were not receiving enough pain care, while pain can be effectively treated in 90–95 percent of terminally ill patients.

What has gone wrong? For one thing, physicians just aren't trained in pallitive care. In one study of eleven hundred oncologists, three out of four admitted they didn't know enough to treat pain! Meanwhile, dying people themselves are trying to exercise some measure of control over the process. A veterinarian in Louisiana named Jim Witcher, who suffers from fast-progressing amyotrophic lateral sclerosis (Lou Gehrig's disease), told me that he most fears choking or smothering to death; he wants help in hastening his death before that happens. But state law, medical ethics, and his family's religious beliefs prohibit it. At the same time, Kitty Rayl in Oregon has access to that state's Death with Dignity Act, which allows her doctor to help her die. But Kitty is in no hurry to leave and wrestles with the timing. The last day I was there to interview her, she said, "I'm sitting up. I have a good book to read. My daughter is coming over with my only grandchild. I'm looking forward to a good day." There you witness the complexity of the issue, played out in one story of a man who wants control and can't have it, and another of a woman who has control but isn't sure she will use it.

In reporting for the series I soon realized that the culture of dying will require a lot of effort in the trenches of our byzantine health care system. Just as every life is a particular life, so each death takes its own course, every family has a different set of issues to deal with, and not everybody has a place to die. It's quite a challenge to create a network that can integrate the social, financial, spiritual, and physical challenges of dying. But there's a model for meeting it. In Birmingham, Alabama, a doctor named Amos Bailey is trying to weave a web of care for the dying and their families. "We are responsible for each other," he says. "That's how the social contract works." The path to our dying depends on the decisions of many individual people. If we can influence those decisions, we can put people on the path to a better death.

I have tried over the last year to imagine my own death. What I want for myself is what everyone wants: a gentle, dignified death, free of pain, attended by the people I love, who love me back. Imagining this, I can more truthfully answer the question people have been asking me since the broadcast aired, "Wasn't it depressing working more than a year on a series about death and dying?" The answer is, "Not at all." The reason is perhaps best illustrated by this story. In the summer of 1922 a Paris newspaper concocted an elaborate scenario for its readers: an American scientist announces the world will end, or at least that such a huge part of the continent will be destroyed, and in such a sudden way, that premature death will be the certain fate of hundreds of millions of people. If this prediction were confirmed, the newspaper asks, "What do you think would be its effects on people between the time when they acquired the aforementioned certainty and the moment of apocalypse? . . . [and] what would you do in this last hour?" One of the readers who responded was a young Marcel Proust:

> I think that life would suddenly seem wonderful to us if we were threatened to die as you say. Just think of how many projects, travels, love affairs, studies, it—our life—hides from us, made invisible by our laziness which, certain of a future, delays them incessantly. But let all this threaten to become impossible forever, how beautiful it would become again! Ah, if only the cataclysm doesn't happen this time, we won't miss visiting the new galleries of the Louvre, throwing ourselves at the feet of Miss X, making a trip to India. The cataclysm doesn't happen, we don't do any of it, because we find ourselves back in the heart of normal life, where negligence deadens desire. And yet we shouldn't have needed the cataclysm to love life today. It would have been enough to think that we are humans, and that death may come this evening.

So it may. Meanwhile . . .

—2000

MOYERS ON AMERICA